sexual harassment

sexual harassment

an employer's guide to causes, consequences and remedies

Business & Professional Publishing

estella engelberg-moston
& stephen moston

Published by Business & Professional Publishing
Unit 7/5 Vuko Place
Warriewood NSW 2102 Australia

First published in 1997

The National Library of Australia
Cataloguing-in-Publication entry

Moston, Stephen.
    Sexual harassment in the workplace: an employer's guide
    to causes, consequences and remedies.

    Includes index.
    ISBN 1 875680 35 7.

    1. Sexual harassment. 2. Sex role in the work environment.
    I. Engelberg-Moston, Estella. II. Title.

    658.3045

Printed in Australia by Star Printery Pty Limited
10 9 8 7 6 5 4 3 2 1

Design by Rockin' Doodles

Distribution in Australia by Woodslane Pty Ltd. Business & Professional Publishing books are available through booksellers and other resellers across Australia and New Zealand. For further information contact Woodslane Pty Ltd on ph (02) 9970 5111, fax (02) 99705002 or email info@woodslane.com.au.

This book is dedicated to Enrique Engelberg and Estela Virginia Labadia, a boss and secretary who married, proving that not all office-based romances are bad. It is also dedicated to Ronald and Lilian Moston who manage to work together, despite being married.

contents

acknowledgments

This book would not have been possible without the assistance of many people. We would especially like to thank the many individuals who have contacted us and described their experiences of sexual harassment. Through their frank and detailed accounts we have come to understand the nature of this problem better.

We would also like to thank the organisations who assisted with this book by providing information on policies and their own experiences of dealing with sexual harassment. Thanks also to Paula Ruzek from *HR Monthly* magazine for her assistance in developing the research materials in the book.

We also acknowledge the assistance given to us by the Australian Research Council, through the provision of Small Grant funds to The University of New South Wales.

Finally, we would like to say a big thank you to Ruth Matheson for her help and encouragement in creating this book.

preface

Sexual harassment is an unusual workplace problem. Few contemporary issues can evoke such polarised attitudes. To some it is a serious problem, requiring draconian actions with implications for all personal relationships within the workplace. Yet to others it is an issue that is both trivial and humorous. When asked their views on sexual harassment, many men state that they are in favour of it and wish that someone would harass them!

These differing positions are, in part, due to the different ways in which we understand what is meant by sexual harassment. Some emphasise the sexual, some remember to emphasise the harassment. In this book, it will be argued that issues of definition are central to understanding the causes of sexual harassment and also towards preventing it.

This book focuses on issues of sexual harassment in Australia, although many of the observations and recommendations are also applicable to other countries such as the UK, New Zealand and the US. These countries have had similar histories in the development of legislation to deal with sexual harassment.

Most of the research material cited is from the UK and the US. Even though Australia has some of the most advanced laws on sexual harassment in the world (noting that there is still some room for improvement), this is not a topic that has attracted a great deal of empirical research. Academics have shied away from the topic, as have private organisations and government bodies. In many cases this is because there has been too much emphasis on the sexual and consequently little interest in meddling in issues that are seen as personal concerns. A major theme of this book is that sexual harassment is an issue that cannot be dismissed so lightly. It is a problem that has significant effects on organisations and their productivity. The focus here is thus on the role of organisations in understanding and dealing with sexual harassment, rather than focusing on its effects on individuals.

The current legislation in Australia means that it is no longer possible for organisations to pretend that the topic does not exist. There is a requirement that they take steps to safeguard their workers by trying to eliminate sexual harassment. Where the weaknesses of the legislation become apparent is in trying to determine exactly which steps should be taken. In essence, the legislation passes the responsibility for dealing with sexual harassment onto organisations. They must draw up their own policies and decide what other actions to take. Unfortunately, no advice is given on how to assess whether such interventions have been effective. We hope that *Sexual Harassment* will shed some light on the topic and assist organisations in addressing this problem.

part one

An old problem with a new name

chapter one

The origins of sexual harassment as a workplace issue

Sexual harassment is one of the most hotly debated contemporary workplace issues. To some it is an issue that detrimentally affects a large number of working people, yet to others it is an example of a minor problem being blown out of proportion by a politically active minority. This situation has not been helped by media coverage of the topic, which has featured a succession of increasingly bizarre stories, often covered more for titillation rather than their actual significance. While these problems are characteristic of many other issues, they are especially significant within the context of sexual harassment since it is a relatively new issue and for many people opinion formation is still at an early stage.

The origins of sexual harassment

Although sexual harassment is apparently a new problem, it is in fact only a new name for a very old problem. Over the last few centuries, stories of workers (both real and fictional accounts) have featured behaviours that would now be classified as sexual harassment. For example, in *Les Miserables,* Victor Hugo describes how one of his protagonists (Fantine) is hounded from her workplace when she rejects the sexual advances of a foreman. The behaviours described in such works do not substantially differ from those descriptions given by modern workers, except that now there is an acknowledgment that such behaviours are wrong and no longer acceptable. Previously, though common and unwanted, such behaviours were more likely to be accepted as part of working life. This has led some writers to observe that sexual harassment is a problem with a short past, but a long history.

It is impossible to consider sexual harassment without some reference to the changing patterns of workforces within industrialised countries over the last century. An increasing number of women have entered the workforce and have gradually made advances towards equality in employment conditions. This has caused friction with the established (male) workforce, who, threatened by change, began to discriminate against newcomers who were different. Sex is the most salient dimension by which we categorise people—there is evidence that children become aware of sex differences and start behaving in a sex-typed way before they are even able to speak. Consequently, when threatened by a new influx of workers, the male workforce began to discriminate against newcomers on the basis of their sex.

Within most historical frameworks sexual harassment is seen as an aspect of sexual discrimination against women and parallels can be drawn with other forms of discrimination, such as racial or religious discrimination. With all such discrimination a single salient characteristic of the newcomer is identified and used as a basis for distinguishing between 'us' and 'them'.

Traditionally, sexual harassment has been conceptualised as a problem for women. However, in what some might regard as an ironic twist, because of rules against sexual discrimination, legislation allows for both women and men to be victims of harassment. Although this is often regarded as a token step, it is in fact a reasonable precaution, since (as we will discover later in *Sexual Harassment*) it is clearly the case that both women and men can and do experience sexual harassment.

The term 'sexual harassment' was first employed in the late 1970s, coming to widespread attention with the publication of Lin Farley's pioneering book, *Sexual Shakedown* (1978). Soon after its publication, the US feminist lawyer Catharine MacKinnon published a book called *Sexual Harassment of Working Women* (1979). These two books were to prove highly significant, elevating the topic to that of a serious social problem. The main landmarks in the development of sexual harassment as a social issue are summarised in Table 1-1.

Table 1-1 *A brief history of sexual harassment*

1975	It is believed that the term 'sexual harassment' is coined about now. The first recorded surveys of 'sexual harassment' take place in the US.
	Working Women United Institute conducts a survey of 155 women in a region of New York. Seventy per cent of subjects report having experienced sexual harassment at least once, and 92 per cent say they think it is a serious problem. Even women who say they have not experienced it consider it a serious problem.
1976	The surveys continue. Notable examples include *Redbook* magazine's survey of its readers. A staggering 9000 readers reply. Eighty-eight per cent of those respondents report having experienced some form of sexual harassment.
	Awareness of sexual harassment increases in the US. Feminists are pivotal to this development. Sexual harassment is seen as a woman's problem.
1978	Lin Farley's book, *Sexual Shakedown: The Sexual Harassment of Women on the Job*, is published. This book is to become a landmark text, exposing real cases of harassment endured by women. Farley is also one of the first to put forward a definition of sexual harassment. In her definition, harassment is conceptualised as male behaviour directed towards women .
1979	Feminist legal scholar Catharine MacKinnon publishes her book, *Sexual Harassment of Working Women*, which becomes another landmark text. MacKinnon defines sexual harassment as an instance of sex discrimination and distinguishes two main types of sexual harassment: *quid pro quo* where a threat or bribery is implied, and hostile environment. Her ideas are influential in shaping future US sexual harassment legislation.
1980	The Equal Employment Opportunities Commission (EEOC) in the US defines and publishes guidelines on sexual harassment.
1981	One of the largest and most comprehensive surveys on all aspects of sexual harassment at work is conducted by the US Merit Systems Protection Board (USMSPB). This study, which surveys nearly 24 000 federal employees, reveals that sexual harassment is an important problem, experienced by men and women, and that it is highly costly.

is estimated that sexual harassment issues have cost the US Government nearly US$200 million in the two-year period covered by the study, a figure that excludes litigation costs.

1982   First large university studies are conducted in the US—one such key study is conducted by Donna Benson and Gregg Thomson at Berkeley.

1984   In Australia, the *Sex Discrimination Act* defines sexual harassment as an instance of sex discrimination.

1985   In Los Angeles, psychologist Barbara Gutek conducts a large-scale telephone study about the nature and prevalence of sexual harassment among workers living in the area. Her findings are published in her book, *Sex and the Workplace*. Gutek is one of the first to suggest a theory about the causes of sexual harassment. Her study remains one of the largest (in terms of sample size) and most informative about sexual harassment.

1988   The results of the second USMSPB study are published. Sexual harassment continues to be a serious problem among federal workers. The cost to the government is estimated as having increased to over US$260 million in the two-year period covered by the study (1985–87).

        The publication *Working Woman* conducts a survey of top American private companies—it is estimated that sexual harassment costs a typical *Fortune 500* company some US$6.7 million per annum.

1991   The Anita Hill–Clarence Thomas hearings take place. Prior to his appointment to the US Supreme Court, Hill had accused Thomas of sexual harassment. Although she loses the case, her accusations spark furious debate and increase the visibility of the issue.

1992   In Australia, the *Sex Discrimination Act* 1984 is amended. Important changes include the removal of the requirement that the victim prove that disadvantages were experienced before making a complaint of sexual harassment.

1994   Police Minister Terry Griffiths is accused of sexual harassment by several women who worked with him. The case sparks media attention and debate in Australia, similar to that seen in the US during the Hill–Thomas case.

1996   Sexual harassment cases continue to be filed. More cases are being heard from male victims and of homosexual harassment.

1996   In Australia, the Federal Sex Discrimination Commissioner launches a new voluntary national Code of Practice to assist employers in preventing sexual harassment.

Sexual harassment myths

As with many offences of a sexual nature (most notably rape), research has shown that men and women often hold attitudes that do not accurately reflect the nature of such offences. Generally, people can hold mistaken beliefs about both the per-petrators and victims of offences, including issues such as why offences are committed. For example, a rape 'myth' would be that many victims invited attack by dressing provocatively. Because sexual harassment is a relatively new public issue, it is not surprising to discover that here too, many people hold mistaken views about those involved in such offences. Since these views are inaccurate perceptions, they are collectively referred to as 'myths'—that is, views that have little or no basis in fact. As we will show in *Sexual Harassment,* many of these beliefs are held by important public officials, including some judges.

Myths and realities

Here is a summary of the most commonly stated myths about sexual harassment.

Myth 1: It is attraction gone wrong

Sexual harassment is viewed as a mistaken reaction to normal courtship rituals. The fault lies with the overly sensitive 'victim'. This view was often voiced when media attention on this topic was in its infancy. Many men simply could not see what the fuss was about. One notable example of this belief's expression was by a judge in the US *(Miller* v. *Bank of America). Playboy* magazine (not surprisingly) has en-dorsed this view, suggesting that women like to receive sexual attention and that complainants must therefore be overly sensitive.

The reality

If this myth were true then we would expect the people involved to be of similar ages and backgrounds, and also unattached, as would be consistent with the establishment of non-harassing relationships. Further, we would not expect those receiving such attention to feel humiliated or offended and the 'suitor' would stop the harassing behaviour following rejection.

Myth 2: Only attractive women are harassed

This view is consistent with the view that harassment is a matter of sexual attraction. A plaintiff in Alabama lost her court case in which she complained she had received sexual harassment because the judge considered her to be unattractive. His logic was that it was not credible that an unattractive woman would be harassed.

The reality

Attractiveness is an irrelevant issue, since sexual harassment is not about courtship or the development of romantic relationships.

Myth 3: Women exploit their sexuality at work

Women 'dress to kill' in the office and then complain when someone compliments them, wolf-whistles or tries to establish a relationship.

The reality

Some men hold the view that the primary reason women enter the workforce is to find a husband. This view is obviously simplistic and ignores the fact that most women work out of either financial necessity, or because they enjoy work and want to develop a career. This view also ignores the fact that most women workers are congregated together in professions or occupations dominated by members of their own sex. Where women do work in male-dominated occupations they are often viewed as threatening, rather than appealing.

Myth 4: Sexual harassment is rare and the media has inflated it out of proportion

As we will discover, many senior managers have expressed the belief that sexual harassment does not happen in 'their' workplaces.

The reality

Incidence studies suggest that sexual harassment is highly prevalent across most workplaces and that managers are out of touch with the problems of their workers.

Myth 5: It's a personal problem

It has been suggested that sexual harassment arises from personal conflicts, or where one person is unnecessarily sensitive to the comments or behaviour of others.

The reality

Shifting the blame for sexual harassment onto the person being harassed is a convenient tactic, absolving the employer of any responsibility. It is difficult to legislate for personal feuds. Current legislation, however, places the responsibility for dealing with sexual harassment firmly with employers, making it a *personnel* issue, not a *personal* issue.

Myth 6: A woman can stop unwanted advances if she wants to

The victim of harassment can prevent further unwelcome behaviours by taking action against the harasser. This might include being assertive and telling the person that their behaviour is unwelcome.

The reality

This is another misconception that has often been aired. Once again, the responsibility both for being harassed and for ending the harassment is shifted to the victim. Victims are often powerless to take action against harassers and can risk sanctions for whistleblowing (for example, a factory floor worker criticising her foreman risks losing her employment). Silence should not be equated with consent.

Myth 7: People make up stories of harassment to gain huge compensation sums

This myth is self-explanatory.

The reality

While it is certainly possible that people may make unjustified accusations, the rewards (financial and personal) for doing so are, at best, minimal. It is far more likely that even people telling the truth will be disbelieved and ridiculed.

Myth 8: 'Nice' women are not harassed

Women who are harassed must have invited attention, perhaps by the way they dressed or behaved. For example, a woman who is assertive or open about sexual matters has encouraged advances.

The reality

As with rape myths, this suggests that certain types of person have invited harassment by their own behaviour. Once again, the myth shifts blame onto the victim, absolving both the organisation (and the harasser) of any moral responsibility.

Myth 9: It is only sexual harassment if there is some visible consequence for non-compliance

For a person to claim they have been harassed, they would need to demonstrate objective undesirable consequences arising from harassment.

The reality

Early definitions of sexual harassment included a requirement that there be some tangible consequences for the victim, such as demotion or dismissal. Today this requirement has been dropped, as some consequences—such as hostile working environments—are often hard to measure objectively.

Myth 10: If the woman had a previous relationship with her 'harasser' then it cannot be harassment

Sexual attentions from someone you have permitted such attentions from in the past do not qualify as harassment, despite indications that they are unwelcome.

The reality

The prior relationship between the parties is irrelevant, as with rape cases. An example here might be that of the manager who uses their power within the organisation to coerce a junior colleague into continuing or extending a relationship against that colleague's will.

A typical case of sexual harassment

Opinions on sexual harassment may have been influenced by a series of sensational media accounts of harassment. Many of the cases featured so prominently undoubtedly help to create an impression that the problem is either trivial, or one that has been blown out of all proportion. One notable recent example featured a US teacher who brought charges against a seven-year-old pupil who had tried to kiss one of the girls from his class during a break period. In many ways this case highlights the absurdity of existing legislation since, even though the case was subsequently dropped, it was given sufficient credence to bring it to the attention of the courts and the media.

In order to put the problem into some perspective we conclude this introductory chapter by featuring a case study of the experiences of one woman (Box 1-1). This person had experienced a variety of forms of sexual harassment over the years and had tried to confront her problems in a number of different ways, ranging from ignoring the problem to taking direct action against a particular harasser. Her case depicts a variety of forms of harassment and its core elements will be recognised by many workers. The account has not been altered in any way, other than to remove details that might identify the author.

An old problem with a new name

Box 1-1 *Sexual harassment in the workplace*

I started work at an engineering factory six years ago when I was 18, I was extremely shy and very nervous about what might await me. I worked in an office carrying out administration for about 300 men on the workshop floor (the rest of the office were all men too). From the day I started to the day I left a few months ago I was treated like something from a different planet.

At first, when they had all got over the initial shock of a young woman invading their workplace, the men treated me in either one of two ways (or sometimes a mixture of the two). I was seen as a sweet, innocent, little girl—everyone's pet who had to be protected, especially from the usual swearing which used to punctuate everybody's language, I felt like a little doll who needed wrapping in cotton wool, I certainly wasn't taken seriously at all! This attitude was mostly displayed by older members of staff who obviously viewed me as their surrogate daughter or grand-daughter. This was bad enough in itself but was made even worse when I realised that some of them also saw me as a sex object which felt really disgusting, almost incestuous.

To the younger men I was a cross between some sort of sex symbol who needed to be conquered, and a whore. They would all stare at me as I walked through the shop floor, I was constantly being shouted at and whistled at. Many, when speaking to me, would stare pointedly at my breasts rather than my face.

After I had settled in a little I became fairly friendly with some of the younger men and some of them turned out to be genuinely interested in me as a person (shock, horror!) but unfortunately I still got the feeling that they would talk behind my back in a derogatory fashion, and that they would get carried away by conversations conducted by the cruder element. Anyway, I would occasionally go out with a group of them and I would be the only female there but I rather enjoyed that and we seemed to get on fairly well.

It wasn't until much later when I moved to another workshop within the company and met my current boyfriend who worked on the shop floor that I found out exactly what they thought of me. There was graffiti on the toilet walls about me—the size of my breasts, who had 'fucked me', etc. were all written for all (but me) to see. My boyfriend told me brief details of how everyone 'knew' that I was a slag and gossip had circulated over who I had (supposedly) had sex with, all this because I had tried to be friendly and sociable to a group of men!

By this time I had become a feminist, a few years of the sort of treatment I had put up with meant I would either have done this or gone mad! I tried to challenge the men's attitudes and beliefs and for a while I became rather hostile towards them. I was really sick of being treated like some sort of featherbrained, naive sexual creature. I then got a name for myself for being stand-offish, unsociable etc. I really couldn't win!

The new office I was working in was situated next to a male inhabited computer room and the walls were literally covered with pornographic pictures which I found disturbing and humiliating. Of course the most disturbing thing being that these men were 'normal', fairly intelligent people with wives and children. I objected on many occasions to this revolting display, firstly calmly letting them know that I was upset by the pictures, then resorting to anger and arguments. Nothing worked, they insisted that these pictures were merely there to 'cheer them up' and that I was only jealous anyway, the usual ridiculous arguments. One of these men took great delight into constantly mentioning the pictures and generally making derogatory remarks about women. At first I used to react every time as he made me so extremely angry but eventually I just put up with his ridiculous games.

One of the foremen who worked in the office next to mine was known to keep a cache of pornographic magazines in the drawer of his desk to look at when he was on the night shift, his nickname was actually 'Porno Joe'! Anyway one day I went into his drawer and removed some of these magazines and hid them away. This seems a silly thing to do but it was the only positive action I could possibly have taken. He obviously knew who had taken them but didn't say anything to me. A few days later I discovered that he had been writing rude and very personal notes to the foremen on days about what he would like to do to me and another girl in the office. I read one of these messages and felt sick and humiliated... I wrote a message back to him telling him that I had seen what he had written knowing that this would shock him as he was actually quite shy and certainly wasn't 'at home' in women's company. I also left him a copy of the procedure to be followed in the case of sexual harassment at work which the unions had published. This seemed to stop the messages but obviously it didn't alter people's opinions of me, although they probably thought I was some sort of frigid, jealous monster. Fancy spoiling their fun! They just couldn't realise that I hated them treating me in that way, they really seemed to see me as a totally different species.

An old problem with a new name

Even those who were perfectly polite and friendly treated me like an imbecile; I was working in an office with one other woman and two men, if anyone came in wanting advice or some work to be done they would invariably go to one of the men (we were all the same grade) even waiting for five minutes or more if the man in question was otherwise engaged. Many times they were eventually referred to me because I was the one they should have seen in the first place, they seemed so shocked that I could actually help them.

I went to college one day a week where I was studying for my degree in Business Studies. When anyone found out I was going to college they always assumed I was there to learn typing and shorthand, that is obviously all they presumed I was capable of!!

About a year ago a campaign was started to get rid of pornographic pictures and calendars which 'decorated' the walls of the workshops. I think this was mainly to give a more professional image to visitors etc, rather than to spare the feelings of any poor female who had to walk past them and suffer the embarrassment. However this idea was viewed with absolute horror, these pictures were part of the shop floor, they brightened things up for the workers! The two people who introduced the idea were said to be jealous (the woman) and gay (the man). Needless to say the pictures are still there—they range from women in rather skimpy clothing to shots of bare breasts and gaping vaginas. Charming.

chapter two

What is sexual harassment?

The objectives of this chapter are:

to explore the complexities of defining sexual harassment
to deconstruct the term 'sexual harassment' by breaking it down
into its core components
to examine organisation and government definitions of sexual
harassment
to make suggestions for the formulation of a definition of sexual
harassment.

Definitions of sexual harassment

Despite some recent well-publicised cases, such as the Anita Hill–Clarence Thomas case in the US, and that of Terry Griffiths in Australia, there is still no clear consensus as to the nature of sexual harassment. Even though the term is widely used, interpretations of what is meant by sexual harassment vary considerably. This can be observed at three main levels.

The national level

There are differences in how sexual harassment is defined across countries. Differing perspectives on the topic, as well as legal constraints, inevitably determine that a definition from one country is unlikely to be wholly endorsed in another. It is also worth noting that cultural variations also have an important influence on acknowledging whether sexual harassment exists as a social or organisational problem.

The organisational level

There are also differences in definition between organisations or companies, where behaviour that is tolerated in one workplace is outlawed in another. This may be evident in several ways, such as differing policies between companies in the same geographical region, or the same type of industry (such as competing car manufacturers). Even within a single company, inconsistencies in policy matters can be easily identified—for example, language that is permitted on the shop floor, is not acceptable in the offices of management.

Not surprisingly, given the impact of government legislation on companies, there is a considerable overlap between organisational and legislative definitions. However, they are not equivalent. Some companies may adopt a more stringent policy towards sexual harassment than is required by law, perhaps as part of a wider policy on sexuality in the workplace. For example, some companies forbid any form of sexual relationships between co-workers.

The individual level

Definitions of sexual harassment can also differ at the individual level. One person may find a behaviour undesirable and distressing, but to another the same behaviour may be inconsequential. Psychological research on attitudes towards sexual harassment has shown that in interpreting and defining behaviours as sexual harassment, individuals take into account a large number of factors that are not stipulated in governmental or organisational policies, such as the prior relationships between the protagonists.

To complicate matters even further, definitions have altered over time. For example, in Australia the conditions for establishing that sexual harassment has occurred have altered substantially over the last decade, as will be detailed later in this chapter.

Box 2-1 *How do you define sexual harassment?*

Before reading this chapter, write down your answers to the following questions:

1. What is sexual harassment? How would you explain sexual harassment to someone who has never heard the term before?

2. What is the definition of sexual harassment in your current workplace?

Deconstructing sexual harassment

The *Concise Oxford Dictionary* defines 'to harass' as 'to trouble and annoy continually or repeatedly'. This definition describes harassment as a process, rather than as an isolated event. It is not so clear whether there is intent on the part of the harasser (did the harasser intend to trouble?), or reaction on the part of the harassed (did the harassed feel troubled?). The ambiguity over the term 'sexual harassment' is even more pronounced. In this chapter it will become clear that there are a number of conceptual ambiguities as well as contradictions concerning the definition of sexual harassment. In this section we set out the major conceptual themes and concepts in definitions of sexual harassment. The problems in finding an adequate definition are numerous, including the creation of workable laws. Perhaps the most significant issue is that, in the absence of a single unifying definition, the problem will continue to be trivialised and dismissed as a personal problem for those involved, rather than as a personnel problem that organisations need to address.

To clarify some of the ambiguities inherent in the term sexual harassment, several major conceptual issues present in definitions of sexual harassment can be identified. These topics serve to define the range of behaviours, circumstances and outcomes that determine whether or not sexual harassment can be said to have occurred. While many of the components of definitions of sexual harassment reflect the views and preoccupations of their creators, others have been determined by research focusing on how individuals interpret sexual harassment.

Elements of definitions

Key elements that definitions of sexual harassment may contain are discussed below.

Gender

Sexual harassment was originally identified and given a name by women. It was defined as male behaviour directed at women. This reflects the social context in which the issue of sexual harassment was identified—sexual harassment was seen as an instance of sex discrimination. As Catharine MacKinnon argued, it is a means to deter women from staying in the workforce, and from promotion to higher or more prestigious (powerful) positions. Lin Farley's influential book *Sexual Shakedown* describes sexual harassment as:

> unsolicited nonreciprocal *male* behaviour that asserts a *woman's* sex role over her function as a worker (1978, p. 33; emphasis is ours).

Therefore, sexual harassment only occurs when:

harassers are male, targets are female.

However, this sex specific element ignores three other possible conditions:

harassers are female, targets are male
harassers are male, targets are male
harassers are female, targets are female.

While many feminist writers' definitions still adhere solely to the first of the four possible situations outlined here, most policy definitions are gender neutral, that is, they cover all four possible situations. This noted, sexual harassment is widely seen as a heterosexual, male-to-female problem, despite the fact that same sex harassment has been acknowledged.

Formal Power

At first, sexual harassment was restricted to those situations where there were tangible consequences to the target, such as sacking or demotion. The idea is that only people with formal power could harass because they are the ones in a position to sanction or reward. This view is exemplified by Louise Fitzgerald's definition:

> Sexual harassment consists of the sexualisation of an instrumental relationship through the introduction or imposition of sexist or sexual remarks, requests or requirements, in the context of a formal power differential (1990, p. 38).

Obvious examples here include the manager who sexually harasses a subordinate, such as a secretary. In definitions such as Fitzgerald's, the explicit statement of a power relationship decrees that harassment can only occur in the following condition:

harassers are in a position of formal power over the harassed.

In this situation, there is a relationship in which women are seen as less powerful in organisational hierarchies, reflecting their position in society as a whole. However, there need not be a formal power differential for sexual harassment to occur, in which case we include the following possible situations:

offenders are of equal power to the harassed
offenders are subordinate to the harassed.

It is further possible that these typologies are still inadequate, as they exclude cases in which there is no apparent power differential—for example, in the case of a cab driver and passenger. To include this possibility, a fourth type of harassment can be defined.

There is no formal relationship between the parties.

Although it is now recognised that any individual can harass another, the popular belief is that sexual harassment is perpetrated by people of higher formal power within the organisational hierarchy over a subordinate, and that somehow this harassment is more serious than co-worker harassment.

The issue of formal power and non-harassing sexual relationships is also contentious. Some definitions place no objections to such relationships, as in the following example from the University of New South Wales (UNSW):

> [The University] …has no concern with the private lives of staff or students… unless their conduct adversely affects the study or workplace. [This institution] acknowledges and respects the fact that two people can engage in any kind of verbal, physical or sexual behaviour, if both freely consent to participate.

However, some writers see these relationships as illegitimate and potentially exploitative. For example, in the definition offered above by psychologist Louise Fitzgerald, it is implied that a truly consensual relationship between people of different formal positions is not possible, and while they cannot be forbidden (we are free to pursue romantic or sexual relationships with any other individual), they should be explicitly discouraged. By stating that relationships may be possible, as in the UNSW definition, several potential problems can arise.

For example, how can we determine whether both people have freely consented? It also sets up potentially ambiguous situations, whereby a staff member can seek a romantic relationship with a student or colleague (such as asking a person for a date), but if that person refuses then sexual harassment may be said to have occurred. If they consent, then it has not. This places a strange set of rules on courting rituals, which if taken to extremes, can lead to apparently bizarre behaviour, where it is necessary to seek written permission to ask a person out. Katie Roiphe, in *The Morning After*, comments that in some US universities male professors are in the habit of leaving their office doors open when female students visit them. Not doing so may be an invitation to charges of sexual harassment.

Ultimately, it is the organisation's decision to allow or discourage such relationships. This is a difficult and sensitive problem that deals with the fear of intrusion into individuals' personal lives and with the kinds of behaviour that are correct for an organisation. It is not uncommon for some organisations to confront some situations by transferring one partner, or even asking them to resign.

Intention

Intention rarely features as an issue in definitions of sexual harassment—emphasis is on reaction. In cases where intention *is* addressed, two possible situations are left:

the initiator intended to harass
the initiator did not mean to harass.

The omission of intention is largely a political strategy, whereby the victims are empowered to define sexual harassment.

Reaction/perception

The reaction of the person who has been 'harassed' is central in almost every definition of sexual harassment. A person is sexually harassed if they feel that they have been sexually harassed. Hence the inclusion of the words *unwanted, unwelcome* and *unreciprocated* in most definitions. Our key concept is thus:

sexual harassment causes offence to the individual.

Feeling harassed is seen as sufficient—but is it necessary? What if a person does not feel harassed by, or is ambivalent about, someone else's behaviour? Writers Edward Lafontaine and Leslie Tredeau's definition states that harassment can occur anyway. They write that sexual harassment includes:

> any action occurring within the workplace whereby women are treated as the objects of the male sexual prerogative. Furthermore, given that women are invariably oppressed by these actions, all such treatment is seen to constitute sexual harassment irregardless of whether the victim labels it as problematic. (1986, p. 435).

In which case, sexual harassment may be said to occur even when:

it does not cause offence.

Accepting this argument suggests that the actions had to be intended to be harassing, for how can we condemn behaviour which is neither intended to be harassing nor perceived as such? It is for these reasons that the issues of perception and intention are deeply interrelated.

Standards of correct behaviour

Typically, it is not possible to define a behaviour as inherently offensive or unacceptable, when there are no universal standards of what is good and what is bad (with the exception of extreme forms of exploitation which will be described later). Having a myriad of beliefs and attitudes is what makes us unique individuals. To establish a workable definition, it is necessary to determine a set of standards that defines a context of behaviour.

In general, it is not possible to make a complaint of harassment after one isolated instance, unless the behaviour is so serious (as in the case of physical sexual assault) that intention need not be proven. With very few exceptions, sexual harassment is a process, not an event. Most policy definitions adhere to what is known as 'the reasonable person standard', a clause that specifies that the behaviour in question would have been perceived as harassment by 'a reasonable person', and not just the complainant. This is intended to account for those actions that could have been meant as *bona fide* on the part of the initiator, and as a vehicle for preventing abuses on the part of the complainant. As the US EEOC compliance manual (the handbook for investigating sexual harassment cases) states, '…the law should not serve as a vehicle for vindicating the petty slights suffered by the hypersensitive' (cited in Petrocelli and Repa, 1992, p. 15).

There is currently some debate as to whether the legal standard should be that of a 'reasonable person', or of a 'reasonable woman'. Research has shown that the majority of sexual harassment complainants are women and that women are more easily offended or affected by sexual or sexist behaviour. Given these findings, some feminists believe that it is women's perceptions and not men's that should be taken into account. We will delve into this issue further in the section on individual perceptions and attitudes. This leaves us with two possible conditions necessary for sexual harassment to have occurred:

it causes offence to a reasonable person

it causes offence to a reasonable woman.

Frequency

The word 'repeated' features in many definitions, largely to emphasise that sexual harassment usually unfolds as a process, creating a hostile and unpleasant environment. The problem with accepting that it has to be repeated is that certain coercive or violent behaviours need only occur once. Therefore, the term repeated should be used with care. Definitions can emphasise one of two possibilities:

harassing behaviours are repeated
repetition is irrelevant.

If repetition is irrelevant, or not discussed, then even a single incident may be a cause for complaint.

Consequences to the harassed

Formal definitions of sexual harassment often stress that the behaviours have direct consequences for the harassed person, including personal distress, poor working conditions or loss of employment. In many feminist writings it is emphasised that the aim of harassment is to oppress women, to drive them out of the workforce, thus eroding economic independence and advancement. Catherine MacKinnon, one of the first feminists to define and articulate a theory of sexual harassment notes:

> sexual harassment exemplifies and promotes employment practices which disadvantage women in work (especially occupational segregation) and sexual practices which intimately degrade and objectify women. In this broader perspective, sexual harassment at work undercuts women's potential for social equality in two interpenetrated ways: by using her employment position to coerce her sexually while using her sexual position to coerce her economically (1979, p. 9).

As Louise Fitzgerald states (1990), sexual harassment was initially thought to be limited to situations where women could lose their jobs, but it has evolved over time to include any deliberate or repeated sexual behaviour that is unwelcome, as well as behaviours that are hostile, offensive or degrading. This is stated in the EEOC (1980) definition, which has become a yardstick for many others:

Unwelcome sexual advances, requests for sexual favours and other verbal or physical conduct of a sexual nature constitute harassment when

1. submission to such conduct is made either explicitly or implicitly a term or condition of an individual's employment;
2. submission to or rejection of such conduct by an individual is used as the basis for employment decisions affecting such an individual; or
3. such conduct has the purpose or effect of substantially interfering with an individual's work performance or creating an intimidating, hostile or offensive working environment.

This definition differentiates between behaviour which is coercive (*quid pro quo*, points 1 and 2) and that which results in a hostile environment (point 3), drawing on MacKinnon's theory and describing sexual harassment as a example of sex discrimination.

To restate, in some definitions sexual harassment occurs only if:

the person harassed suffers some tangible consequence of harassment.

The current Australian Human Rights and Equal Employment Opportunity Commission (HREOC) definition has modified this requirement. Australian law had previously required the complainant to establish that they were disadvantaged and had experienced actual damage as a result of rejecting the harassment, or had reasonable grounds for believing that a rejection would subject them to a detriment or disadvantage. This is no longer necessary, although the issue of disadvantage and damage can still be relevant to determining the amount of damages to be awarded. Consequently, the sole condition that determines whether sexual harassment has occurred would be that:

sexual harassment occurs if the target feels offended/embarrassed.

Setting

Where does sexual harassment occur? There are two possible situations, centring on whether it is seen as occurring on a set territory, such as the office, or whether it can occur in any location where work colleagues may come into contact, including locations such as the home. That is, the setting of sexual harassment can be seen in two ways:

it is a workPLACE problem
it is a working RELATIONSHIP problem.

An organisation's concern rests with the relations among their employees and it is often unclear what their standing or power to act would be if an employee is harassed by a member of another organisation, or if an employee harasses someone employed elsewhere. This position is particularly difficult when clients or contract workers are involved.

Harassment can occur between individuals sharing a working relationship or in a working context, however fleeting this relationship may be. In this respect, the HREOC states that:

> Amendments make it clear that it is unlawful for employers, employees, contract workers, commission agents or partners to sexually harass another workplace participant in a mutual place of work or where they carry out functions related to their work [s.28B(6) and (7)].

This broader coverage will ensure that:

> Sexual harassment at work is made unlawful no matter what particular employment or professional relationship exists between people. Even if an employment relationship does not exist, sexual harassment can occur if a contractual relationship exists (such as contract workers or consultants). For example, it is now unlawful for a partner to harass a contract worker.
>
> Sexual harassment is unlawful in situations in connection with work, for example where work is performed away from the workplace, such as whilst on business trips or training programs.

Sexual or sexist behaviour

The term sexual harassment is often used to describe sexual behaviour exclusively and is closely tied in with widespread beliefs about its causes (sexual interest). Although sexual harassment was defined as an instance of sex discrimination in its early days, beliefs about (hetero)sexual motives, including (hetero)sexual attraction 'gone wrong' permeated popular thought. US educationalist Phyllis Franklin and her colleagues were among the first to include gender-based behaviour within a sexual harassment definition. They write:

> For many the most difficult kind of behaviour to include as a form of sexual harassment was verbal harassment or abuse, by which students often mean pejorative (sexist or stereotyped) assumptions made about women as a group... by persons in positions of authority. Such behaviour seems qualitatively different from the other items on the list. It is this kind of behaviour that we are designating 'gender harassment'. ...The forms are often verbal—statements and jokes that reveal stereotypical discriminatory attitudes, for example. The offender may describe women as fickle, irrational, and hysterical or may define them exclusively in terms of their sexual attractiveness and functioning. Also damaging are expressed or implied 'positive' assumptions that women are nurturing, self-sacrificing, intuitive, closer to nature (1981, pp. 4–5).

The view of sexual harassment as 'sexual' prevailed longer, and it was not until 1993 that the EEOC supplemented the original guidelines, stating that the 'hostile environment' prohibition also includes offensive sex-related conduct that is not specifically sexual in nature, that is, *gender* harassment. The updated guidelines state that gender harassment is 'verbal or physical conduct that denigrates or shows hostility or aversion'. Sexual harassment may thus include:

sexual behaviour

sexist behaviour.

The HREOC definition continues to emphasise the sexual element, where sexual harassment is defined as unwelcome sexual advances, unwelcome requests for sexual favours or other unwelcome conduct of a sexual nature. 'Unwelcome conduct of a sexual nature' includes the making of a statement of a sexual nature to a person, or in a person's presence, whether orally or in writing.

Examples of behaviours

At their most simplistic and ineffective level, some definitions consist of lists of behaviour. Others do not give examples at all. Those that do, generally describe physical forms and unwanted comments of a sexual or sexist nature. The UNSW provides the following examples:

- offensive jokes, verbal abuse of a sexual type
- leering or offensive gestures
- repeated or irrelevant reference to a person's gender or private life
- inappropriate touching, pinching, squeezing, tickling, repeated bumping or brushing up against the victim
- demands for sexual activity accompanied by threats of loss of job, denial of promotion, failure in course
- offers of rewards for sexual favours
- sexual or physical assault.

How many people and how can they be harassed?

Definitions often focus on direct, one-to-one actions that occur with both parties present. It is important to stress that harassment can occur in writing, as well as verbally, and not necessarily in the recipient's presence. The HREOC states that:

> The amendments make clear that statements need not 'concern that person'. A prevailing atmosphere of sexual harassment in the form of generally offensive sexual comments and behaviour could constitute sexual harassment [s.28A(2)].

This considerably widens the possible scope for cases of sexual harassment. Definitions can thus stress that:

sexual harassment is a one-to-one process
sexual harassment can be directed at more than one person, or to no one in particular.

Further complications

So far we have discussed the major elements of definitions in isolation, each concept being treated as though it were an independent factor, to show the variety of factors that may or may not be present in any given definition. For example, one definition may specify the gender of the parties involved, while another does not. Definitions of sexual harassment, however, are rarely comprised of single defining elements—most definitions incorporate a number of elements.

A further complication concerning the definition of sexual harassment is the way in which the various concepts can be combined together. In some cases the 'mixing' of concepts can create ambiguities and contradictions that are not easily reconciled. For example, many definitions of sexual harassment state that there need not be any detrimental consequences for the victim of harassment. It is sufficient that the victim feels that they have been harassed. This concept is a key feature of most current definitions and was included to allow cases in which women experience hostile working environments where objective consequences (such as demotion) cannot be easily proven. In isolation, this concept appears to present few problems. However, a complication arises when the victim of sexual harassment is male. Some writers argue that men cannot be the victim of sexual harassment because as a rule they cannot suffer any objective consequences of harassment. This is clearly a contradictory position: a woman need not suffer any objective consequences, yet a man must. This type of contradictory position clearly stems from political interpretations of sexual harassment.

Box 2-2 *Analysing definitions of sexual harassment*

In Box 2-1 you were asked to write down your own definition of sexual harassment, together with that put forward by your current employer. Which of the above elements have been included in these definitions? Has either definition effectively excluded some types of harassment?

Try to map out these definitions using the elements discussed in this chapter. It is likely that your company's definition will probably overlap considerably with at least one of the other definitions featured. Most current definitions are highly derivative, being developed from one former definition (the EEOC definition is especially prevalent as a base). p. 23-24.

Individual definitions of sexual harassment

There are two basic approaches when trying to devise a definition of sexual harassment. The *empirical* approach is to ask individuals how they personally define sexual harassment. The alternative is to base a definition on elements of underlying theoretical assumptions about the causes of sexual harassment—for example, by assuming that harassment stems from sexism. This approach is termed *a priori*.

Psychological research in the 'individual appraisal process' bloomed in the 1980s and continues to be popular, particularly in the US. This reflects both positively and negatively on the state of society's attitudes towards sexual harassment; positively, because any research indicates interest in a social problem, but negatively, because attitudinal research has become virtually the only kind of sexual harassment research conducted. There are several, largely pragmatic, reasons that this is the case. Attitudinal research can often be carried out with little or no funding, and it is often the only form of research that is permissible! Firms are particularly reticent to carry out systematic research on sexual harassment for fear that the results might prove costly and/or embarrassing. This is an issue that will be examined in greater detail in Chapter 3.

Louise Fitzgerald has suggested that empirical research studies analysing individual perceptions fall into three categories. The first involves the evaluation of given behaviours, the second involves evaluation of fictitious scenarios describing socio-sexual behaviour, and, finally, the direct assessment of attitudes and beliefs about sexual harassment.

Evaluation of behaviours

This type of research involves presenting individuals with simple lists of behaviours, such as 'sexual comments/jokes', 'touching/stroking', 'invitations for dates' and asking them to evaluate whether any of these constitute sexual harassment. Alternatively, individuals are asked to rate these actions in terms of how offensive they are, how threatening, how embarrassing, and so forth. Overall, such studies suggest that there is a gender gap between men and women in defining sexual harassment. Women are more likely to see sexual harassment than men, in particular where the behaviours are more ambiguous, though opinions tend to converge with respect to *quid pro quo* harassment and actions involving physical assault (see Chapter 3 for more information on these types of harassment). Such results appear to vindicate the use of the 'reasonable woman' standard in determining whether sexual harassment has occurred, although this conclusion may be somewhat premature. There are a number of weaknesses in this style of research, not least of which is the absence of any context to the behaviours listed. With the exception of assault , bribery or coercion, sexual behaviour *per se* is not good or bad unless other elements are specified (for example, complimenting someone on their appearance).

Evaluation of 'sexual harassment scenarios'

Another way of trying to derive a definition of sexual harassment is to carry out studies in which individuals are presented with a variety of scenarios in which elements of the stories are systematically varied. These elements include:

- *characteristics of the sender*, that is the person who may or may not be sexually harassing another (factors such as the person's marital status and organisational power have been studied)
- *characteristics of the recipient*, that is, the person who may or may not be experiencing sexual harassment (here, features such as the person's organisational status or clothing have been examined)
- *behaviour/actions*—a variety of potentially harassing behaviours have been examined (such as displaying pornography or touching)
- *contexts*, where additional factors are introduced into the scenarios, such as the existence of a prior personal relationship between the two characters.

These stories are then given to participants, who are asked to evaluate issues such as 'Was the behaviour sexual harassment?' (and sometimes asked to rate the degree of harassment on a scale), 'Was the behaviour serious/offensive?', and so forth. Researchers also take demographic and/or personality data from the person doing the rating to see whether this influences judgments.

US researcher Mary Ellen Reilly and her colleagues (1982) pioneered this kind of study by using 'the factorial survey technique', which uses a computer program to generate all the possible combinations of several judgment elements.

The elements that raters seem to take into account are:

- type of behaviour (physical behaviour is seen as more negative and serious)
- whether the harasser has formal power over the victim
- the behaviour of the victim
- the prior relationship of the parties involved.

Actions from a superior are seen as worse than those from a co-worker, possibly because people associate the idea of sexual harassment with tangible (or economic, as opposed to psychological) consequences. As a superior has power over the other person's standing in the organisation, his harassment is seen as more serious than that of a colleague with no power to affect the person's career.

Raters take into account how the harassed party reacts—if a person reacts negatively and if she makes this clear to the harasser, her plight will receive more sympathy. Somehow it seems that people are not prepared to believe a complaint if (a) the complaint is not immediate, or, (b) the harassed party does not complain about the behaviour to the harasser. This issue is explored in depth in Chapter 6.

The notion that harassment is sexual and a by-product of sexual attraction still prevails in most people's beliefs—if the parties are seen to have been friendly or romantically involved in the past, raters will see less harassment, which is consistent with the notion that once consent is given, it cannot be withdrawn. However, the most robust finding of this research is that women see more sexual harassment than men in ambiguous circumstances and have broader definitions and less acceptance of sexual harassment. Some researchers have found that gender differences in attitudes are influenced by individual differences such as religiosity, locus of control or endorsement of feminist beliefs. They are also influenced by personal experience. Because women are more likely to be the targets of sexual victimisation in general, it is not surprising that women are readier to label potentially harassing behaviours as harassment. It is interesting to note that when the sex-role attitudes of those evaluating the scenarios are taken into account, gender differences are not clear cut—individuals with traditional sex-role attitudes are more tolerant of sexual harassment regardless of their sex or individual experience.

It is also worth noting that studies showing gender differences feature university students, and at least one study which sampled employed people has largely failed to find any clear gender gap in attitudes. It is thus possible that students (particularly women students, in this regard at least) may hold attitudes that differ from the general working population.

Attitude scales studies

This type of research begins with the formulation of theoretical statements about the nature of sexual harassment and related issues, and then asks individuals to rate them. Fitzgerald gives some examples of statements of this kind:

'I believe sexual harassment is a serious social problem'
'Most people who file complaints of sexual harassment are just trying to get the person in trouble'
'Most complaints of sexual harassment are false'
'Much of what is called sexual harassment is just normal sexual interplay between adults'.

Ratings of such statements have shown again that women see more harassment than men and consider it a more serious problem. However, the ratings and the statements chosen by researchers also show how an individual's judgments are a complex mixture of perceptions about the world, the general attitudes of the society in which they live, the current political and social context and the entrenched belief of the heterosexuality of sexual harassment.

The impact of individual attitudes studies

The most notable consequence of the issues raised by individual attitude research on social and legal policy is the development of 'the reasonable woman' standard, which conforms to the feminist conceptualisation of sexual harassment as women's victimisation. According to this standard, behaviour should be evaluated from the perspective of a woman, given that women are more often the recipients of offensive sexual behaviour. In 1991, in the *Ellison* v. *Brady* hearing (cited in Fitzgerald 1994), the US 9th Circuit noted:

> Conduct that many men consider unobjectionable may offend many women... Men who are rarely victims of sexual assault, may view sexual harassment in a vacuum, without a full appreciation of the social setting or the underlying threat of violence that a woman may perceive.

There is debate surrounding this issue. Some believe it is better to define certain behaviours as harassment regardless of attitudes, but this overlooks the fact that most sexual harassment is ambiguous and is heavily dependent on context. In Australia, the HREOC has adopted the reasonable person standard, apparently because no local systematic research has been conducted to prove that the reasonable woman standard is more satisfactory, and in line with the 'gender neutral' tone of the sexual harassment definition.

Gender differences notwithstanding, this standard may reflect a (hetero)sexist attitude and implies that men are not as capable as women of seeing sexual harassment when it has indeed occurred. In effect, the underlying premise for such an assertion is that men may have a different set of moral values to women, something that is not supported by current psychological research. Overall, research shows little variation in moral codes between the sexes, with arguments over 'different voices' of moral thinking relying solely on anecdotal and unquantifiable data.

The methodological weaknesses of attitudinal studies bear one further comment. Their limitations are so apparent that many writers are able to dismiss them effectively from consideration. For example, they portray the participants in scenarios as passive and largely mindless. In isolating variables for the sake of methodological simplicity, researchers ignore the range of factors that interact to shape our interpretations of events. Individually, we can show that certain factors may affect ratings of harassment, but we do not know if these variables are additive in any way, or whether they negate each other.

Is there a satisfactory definition of sexual harassment?

In this chapter a number of different approaches to the definition of sexual harassment have been reviewed. In short, legal/organisational definitions tend to overlook individual experience, while definitions generated by individuals tend to ignore theoretical concerns. The issue of definition is a highly contentious one, with a number of conflicting elements present across the range of definitions. A major concern for organisations in any country will be to adhere to the requirements of their own government. If they then choose to adopt a definition that expands on the legal requirements, this is their prerogative. To adopt a definition that narrows the legal requirements is obviously not an option, although it seems inevitable that in trying to adopt policies on sexual harassment, many firms will, in fact, inadvertently restrict the range of behaviours/situations where sexual harassment can be said to have occurred. Employees are more likely to be familiar with their own companies' policies or guidelines on sexual harassment than with the legal conception. A person may therefore incorrectly believe that they do not have cause for complaint, when in fact they may have just cause.

Although government legislation is the 'bottom-line' for most companies, it is important to recognise that legislation is often changed, particularly when a given policy has been shown to be ineffective or problematic. In adhering to current legislation employers may well help to eliminate some instances of sexual harassment, but while there are still ambiguities and confusions, loopholes will continue to become apparent. Employers should recognise that sexual harassment has a number of serious consequences for the individuals concerned and for the company as a whole (as will be discussed in Chapters 6 and 7). By failing to adopt a perspective on the problem that is broad enough and by merely observing the minimum requirements imposed by law, the negative consequences of sexual harassment will continue to be felt, even though firms may doggedly insist that they do not have a problem.

In Chapter 3 we will discuss the way in which measuring the incidence of sexual harassment is heavily influenced by how it is defined. This chapter has shown that sexual harassment has many different interpretations, many of which are contradictory. The reliability of incidence surveys is thus called into question, given that each survey is effectively concerning itself with a different set of behaviours/circumstances. Furthermore, to base surveys on single questionnaire items such as 'Have you been sexually harassed?' is an entirely meaningless exercise. Put simply, no two interpretations of this question will agree entirely. A one line incidence survey may allow firms to publicly state that they do not have a problem with sexual harassment, but this strategy is one of burying their head in the sand. The problem may well exist, but under another name, and most significantly, it will continue to have negative consequences for all those concerned.

chapter three

How common is sexual harassment?

The objectives of this chapter are:
to examine the incidence of sexual harassment
to outline the steps necessary to the development of reliable surveys
*to suggest ways of classifying and 'measuring' sexual harassment in
    the workplace.*

Why do we need to know the incidence of sexual harassment?

Sexual harassment is not a *personal* problem, it is a *personnel* problem. This was
the conclusion of American writers Constance Backhouse and Leah Cohen in 1982.
In the 1990s this assertion is more a reality than ever. From a legal point of view, as
we saw in Chapter 2, employers have a duty to keep a workplace free from harassment. From a moral point of view, employers owe to their employees a dignified
and respectful working environment, and they owe it to themselves to avoid the
potentially huge financial losses.

Regrettably, there has been a tendency to cut corners for the sake of saving
face. Though it is commendable that an increasing number of organisations are
adopting informal and formal procedures, and informing the workforce about sexual
harassment (usually by distributing pamphlets or holding seminars about sexual
harassment), such approaches may not tackle the problem head-on. The issue here
should not be 'Let's purge the workplace of sexual harassment', but rather 'Let's

find out whether sexual harassment happens at all, how it is manifested, and then find the most sensible, cost-effective way of tackling the problem'.

The first step in this process is a survey of the incidence of (unwanted) sexual behaviours in the workplace. An incidence survey should be given to a representative cross-section of the organisation, not just to personnel or management. Opponents of this strategy may take the cynical stance that conducting an incidence survey may alarm an organisation where sexual harassment is not a problem and cause further havoc in one where it actually happens. In the latter case, complaints may increase as employees make more sense of any unwanted experiences. If this should happen management should not assume that harassment is on the increase, but that employees are exercising their rights and demanding a harassment-free workplace.

In this chapter, we will review findings from influential survey studies and discuss the process of survey construction in the context of organisational efforts to prevent sexual harassment.

Assessing the incidence of sexual harassment

Despite the variations in how sexual harassment is defined, it is apparent that the problem is both persistent and widespread, particularly for women. However, determining just how persistent and widespread it is has been highly problematic. Even though there have been a large number of studies by academic researchers, as well as by organisations themselves, an agreed set of figures concerning the incidence of sexual harassment is still lacking. Here we summarise the findings of several of the most notable incidence studies before proceeding to a discussion of how one might accurately measure the incidence of sexual harassment.

There are two main survey methodologies available to examine the extent of sexual harassment. First, researchers may distribute questionnaires to workers. These questionnaires may specifically address sexual harassment, or questions on this topic may form part of a wider ranging study, for example, on other problems in the workplace. Second, a researcher may examine archival records, such as records of formal complaints or grievances. Such a procedure is less intrusive than a questionnaire-based study, but is prone to a number of major shortcomings, not least of which is the tendency for firms to 'disguise' cases of sexual harassment (see Box 3-1 below). This means that analysing figures based on formal grievances or complaints will produce underestimates. One example of this type of research was reported by Ronni Sandroff, who describes a 1988 study for the American publication *Working Woman*. This study consisted of a survey of personnel managers from 160 corporations, representing 3.3 million employees in the US. The personnel managers reported that complaints of sexual harassment were rare, with only 1.4 complaints per 1000 women. While such figures are seemingly objective, they are unlikely to be reliable, as many cases will go unreported if victims fear they will not be believed or that the offender may take retaliatory action following an accusation—particularly if the harasser is the person's immediate supervisor.

Box 3-1 *The 'reclassification' of sexual harassment*

Claire was a senior executive at a large Australian public company. Following a meeting, a drunken colleague had molested her (and another woman) and chased them from the room, after which they were forced to hide in a toilet cubicle. Her employers accepted her story and took action against the offender. However, the action taken made no reference to her ever having been sexually harassed, with the offender being asked to take early retirement. The offender left the company in apparently amicable circumstances, while the woman who had been harassed was told that her career would be jeopardised if she were to let the truth of the matter be known.

While there was a positive outcome to this case, in that the offender was removed, the way in which it was done clearly gives cause for concern. Companies may go to great lengths to ensure that complaints are never heard in public. Sexual harassment cases are disguised, or reclassified, to such an extent that only those directly concerned know what has happened.

One further problem in attempting to determine the frequency of sexual harassment is that many firms are reluctant to discuss such a sensitive issue. If a study were to show high levels of sexual harassment in a given company, even if that company was committed to eliminating the problem, it would undoubtedly cause a great deal of bad publicity for the company concerned. It is thus not surprising to learn that even when companies have conducted incidence studies, the results are highly confidential. Such problems have greatly hindered the efforts of researchers. It means that organisations are reluctant to participate in studies, unless anonymity can be guaranteed. The extent to which companies 'avoid' the issue of sexual harassment was noted by Sandroff, who found that only 9 per cent of the companies in her study included questions about sexual harassment on employee surveys and only 4 per cent raised it during exit interviews. Sandroff reports that 7 per cent of companies had harassment hotlines, a surprisingly low figure given that part of a settlement against the Goodyear company required the introduction of a free phone number for confidential reports of harassment.

Prevalence figures: some general findings

The most widely reported surveys in the US and the UK suggest that between 33 per cent and 50 per cent of women are victims of sexual harassment at least once in their lives. The percentage is lower for men. A higher percentage of workers have received some form of sexual overture and it is estimated that around 10 per cent of women have quit their jobs because of sexual harassment.

A study in a university setting conducted in the UK revealed similar findings (Stockdale 1986). The authors argue that figures are likely to be an underestimate, as many targets may feel anxious or apprehensive about complaining. In general, people will report less harassment if they are allowed to define sexual harassment themselves. This means that asking a person 'Have you been sexually harassed?' will elicit few endorsements! This immediately highlights an obvious limitation to one of the central tenets of sexual harassment, namely that victim perceptions are crucial to the determination of whether or not an incident is harassment. 'If you feel harassed, then you have been harassed' is the often stated argument. However, without some further information, it appears that many people will not define harassment solely on subjective experiences—an objective definition or set of criteria is clearly required. To base a study of sexual harassment on a single question, such as 'Have you been sexually harassed?', is likely to produce highly unreliable data, probably suggesting that incidence is very low. Unfortunately, the Australian firms interviewed by the authors admitted to assessing the occurrence of sexual harassment by asking this solitary question. In the next section, some major incidence studies carried out in the workplace are summarised and incidence studies in higher education establishments are examined.

Incidence studies in the workplace

Surveys of sexual harassment seldom tackle incidence alone. Attitudes, perceptions, reactions and consequences of sexual harassment are often assessed and interpreted together. This supplementary information is needed to understand the mechanics of sexual harassment. For example, fewer people will report having experienced sexual harassment if they believe management does not take the issue seriously. Surveys which deal with all these issues, if properly constructed and conducted, can offer valuable information about what happens, why it happens and what can be done to prevent it. Below four landmark surveys that were conducted in the US in the 1980s are described. These studies are unusual, in that they have relatively large sample sizes and a reasonable choice of subjects.

The United States Merit Systems Protection Board studies

The largest and one of the most comprehensive studies to date were the two studies conducted by the USMSPB. Both studies were based on written questionnaires that were sent to a representative cross-section of some 13 000 Federal Government workers, both males and females, of whom just over 8 500 responded (a very healthy 85 per cent response rate, given the subject matter). This study was originally conducted in 1980 and repeated in 1987 (published 1981 and 1988 respectively), the latter study resulting in an updated and comparative report.

Despite the relative sampling limitation of the studies (it only sampled employees of the Federal Government), both the surveys and the corresponding reports are thorough and comprehensive. The questions on incidence of sexual harassment tapped the experience of the following seven behaviours:

- actual or attempted rape or assault
- unwanted pressure for sexual favours
- unwanted deliberate touching, leaning over, cornering or pinching
- unwanted sexual looks or gestures
- unwanted letters, telephone calls or materials of a sexual nature
- unwanted pressure for dates
- unwanted sexual teasing, jokes, remarks or questions.

The questions in this study centred on whether the respondents had experienced any of the seven harassment behaviours in the two years prior to the study. Questions typically took the following format. A subject might be asked *'How often have you received any of the following uninvited and unwanted sexual attention during the last 24 months from someone where you work in the Federal Government?'*, with the seven behaviours then being given. Subjects could indicate whether they had experienced the behaviours on a scale from 'never' through to 'once a week or more'.

The questionnaire also included a number of questions concerning sexual behaviour in the workplace, where subjects were asked to state whether they believed an incident constituted sexual harassment. For example, subjects were asked *'We would like to know what you would think if the following happened to you or to someone else at work'*. The seven behaviours were then listed and subjects asked to rate whether it was harassment if committed, by either a superior or a co-worker.

In both surveys, the incidence of female employees having experienced at least one form of sexual harassment was 42 per cent; 15 per cent of the male employees reported being harassed in the first study, and 14 per cent in the second. The most frequently reported individual behaviours were: unwanted teasing, jokes, remarks or questions. The least frequently reported behaviours were actual or attempted rape or assault. Victims of sexual harassment usually experienced more

than one form of harassment—for example, a person might experience both unwanted comments and unwanted touching. In the second study it was found that
workers were more likely to define a set of (sexual) behaviours as sexual harassment. For example, in the 1988 report, over 80 per cent of male and female workers
saw uninvited pressure for dates by a supervisor as sexual harassment, while in 1981
the figure had been lower, at 77 per cent. The main findings of the incidence studies
are shown below in Table 3-1.

Table 3-1 *Forms of sexual harassment experienced by women and men in the
USMSPB studies*

Form of sexual harassment	% of female respondents who claimed they experienced this form of harassment		% of male respondents who claimed they experienced this form of harassment	
	1980	1988	1980	1988
Sexual remarks	33	35	10	12
Suggestive looks	28	28	8	9
Pressure for dates	26	15	7	4
Deliberate touching	15	26	3	8
Pressure for sexual favours	9	9	2	3
Letters and calls	9	12	3	4
Actual or attempted rape or assault	1	0.8	0.3	0.3

These studies were important landmarks in the attempt to measure the
incidence of sexual harassment. The strengths of the studies were the large sample
size and the existence of a follow-up report. This comparative data showed that
attitudes to sexual harassment had changed during the intervening years. The main

limitations of the studies are that the seven harassment categories appear somewhat arbitrary and overlapping (for example, how should a sexual remark in a letter be classified), the subjects are asked to infer the intentions of the harasser ('deliberate touching'), and most importantly, they exclude many possible forms of sexual harassment, including sexist or gender harassment. Such studies are also very costly and require considerable organisational commitment and financial backing.

Gutek's Los Angeles study

Another large and systematic study was conducted by Barbara Gutek, then associate professor of psychology, business administration and executive management at The Claremont Graduate School. Gutek conducted telephone interviews with a representative sample of 1 232 full-time workers (827 women, 405 men) in the Los Angeles area workforce (achieving a 77 per cent response rate to the study). The study also included men and women and assessed the following sexual harassment/sexual behaviour categories:

- complimentary sexual comments
- insulting sexual comments
- complimentary sexual looks/gestures
- insulting sexual looks/gestures
- nonsexual touching
- sexual touching
- pressure for dates with threats of job reprisals
- expected sexual activity with threats of job reprisals.

The questions in Gutek's study were concerned with the respondents' experiences across their working lives. An example question is *'Sometimes on the job, men make comments of a sexual nature that are meant to be compliments. On your present job, have you ever received sexual remarks from a man that he meant to be complimentary?'*. (This question is from the women's version of the questionnaire). The respondents could reply with *Yes*, *No* or *Decline to answer*. Each question was asked concerning the respondents' current job, and across their entire working life. Obviously some of these questions are not necessarily sexual harassment, but simply sexual behaviours in the workplace, and so respondents were also asked if they had labelled such experiences as sexual harassment. Asking questions in such a format produced some interesting data, such as finding that 68 per cent of the women had received complimentary sexual comments at some stage of their lives, but that only 19 per cent ever labelled such behaviour as sexual harassment.

Gutek found that 53 per cent of the female respondents reported at least one instance of what they perceived to be sexual harassment during their working lives, while the corresponding figure for men was 37 per cent. Males and females experiences of social–sexual behaviours that they labelled as sexual harassment are shown in Table 3-2 below.

Table 3-2 *Experience of sexual harassment by males and females in Gutek's study*

Experience of social–sexual behaviours labelled as sexual harassment	% of males	% of females
Complimentary comments	10.4	18.9
Insulting comments	12.1	19.8
Complimentary looks, gestures	8.1	16.2
Insulting looks, gestures	9.6	15.4
Nonsexual touching	3.5	3.6
Sexual touching	12.3	24.2
Expected socialising	7.4	10.9
Expected sexual activity	3.2	7.6

Although this study offers some important insights into the workplace factors associated with sexual harassment, it suffers from a number of significant limitations. Once again, the questionnaire only features a sub-sample of the full range of behaviours that might constitute sexual harassment (for example, pin-ups are not included). The design of the questions is also problematic, as the respondent is being asked to infer the intention of the person initiating the social–sexual behaviours. There were also a large number of apparently trivial questions in the study, particularly those concerning the personality of the respondent and how their personality was perceived by co-workers.

Incidence studies in higher education institutions

Academia has been a fertile ground for surveys of sexual harassment. Studies began in US campuses in the late 1970s, fuelled by increasing student and staff recognition of the negative effect of sexual harassment in the academic community. The first surveys were open-ended exercises in which responses from self-identified victims of sexual harassment were elicited. Not surprisingly, the figures for women were very high. One such open-ended endeavour from 1980 was conducted by Frank Till, who classified the responses of a national sample of college women into five general categories of sexual harassment. Till asked these students to report whether they had received what they considered to be sexual harassment and to relate their experiences in their own words. The categories were as follows:

- gender harassment—generalised sexist remarks and behaviour
- seductive behaviour—inappropriate and offensive, but essentially sanction-free behaviour, that is, with no penalty attached to non-compliance
- sexual bribery—solicitation of sexual activity or other sex linked behaviour by promise of rewards
- sexual coercion—coercion of sexual activity by threat of punishment
- sexual imposition or assault—gross sexual imposition (that is, touching, fondling, grabbing) or assault.

One of the first systematic surveys of US campuses was conducted by Donna Benson and Gregg Thomson in 1982 at the University of California at Berkeley. Here, respondents were given a definition of sexual harassment and then asked whether they had been sexually harassed and to describe the incident. The findings showed that nearly one in three women had experienced some form of sexual harassment during their academic careers. Similarly, another study at East Carolina University asked students whether they had experienced any of seven types of harassment. Thirty three per cent of the women surveyed reported being harassed by male teachers. In 1988, Louise Fitzgerald conducted a large and systematic survey of university women in which she questioned over 2 500 students (women and men) about five different types of sexual harassment, ranging from comments and seductive behaviour to sexual assault, which were derived from Till's typology. Fitzgerald found that approximately half of the women had experienced some form of harassment from persons of formal power (supervisors or tutors) during their academic careers. The most frequently reported behaviour in this and other surveys was gender harassment, but a large number of students also reported experiencing unwanted sexual attention and nearly 10 per cent reported some gross sexual imposition including touching, grabbing and sexual assault. Generally, the most pre-valent forms of harassment identified in academic samples are forms of gender harassment, a kind of harassment often ignored in research questionnaires. Sexual assault and rape appear far less likely, with estimates ranging from 1–10 per cent of students experiencing such behaviours. Reports of harassment from men in this study were almost negligible.

Some problems with existing surveys

There are many other incidence studies that have been conducted over the last 20 years. In most cases, the definition of sexual harassment, structuring of question-naire items and question wording have been consistently inconsistent. Even though the studies do at least show that many people, particularly women, are likely to ex-perience some form of unwanted sexual behaviour either in the workplace or aca-demia, we cannot accurately place a figure on how prevalent sexual harassment might be. The studies that have been carried out to date share a number of important methodological shortcomings that further hinder our attempts to answer this question.

All surveys of sexual harassment reflect a political ideology and this is shown in the way that sexual harassment is defined as well as to whom the survey is given. A survey which is administered only to women, assumes that sexual harass-ment can only happen to women (unless the researchers explicitly state that they are interested in women's experiences only). A survey which asks about the experience of certain behaviours without establishing a context may assume that such behaviours constitute sexual harassment, even when they do not. For example, sexual jokes are not inherently sexual harassment, since an employee may find such jokes highly amusing and inoffensive.

Incidence figures determined by researchers may be unrealistically low if too narrow a definition of sexual harassment is employed, or unrealistically high if the definition is too all-encompassing. They may even be fundamentally incorrect if the definition does not reflect the legal requirements of the state or country in which the study is conducted. Further, as each research team employs a different set of criteria to define sexual harassment, it grows increasingly difficult to integrate findings.

Studies usually feature a group of workers in one particular occupation, or type of work, rather than a representative sample of the workforce. Comparing figures for differing populations is an important step towards understanding the causes of sexual harassment (see Chapter 4), but if the survey methodology and definition is unique to each population, then comparison is impossible. Studies are typically carried out on what is termed 'samples of convenience', that is, groups upon whom a questionnaire can be imposed. For example, studies might feature federal employees or the military—groups whose specific work conditions or circumstances may differ from those of the general working population.

Surveys often consist of a constellation of questions and statements concerning attitudes, perceptions, experiences and consequences of sexual harassment. Terminology used is not always clear, or interpreted equally by the respondents—just what is a 'suggestive comment'? Considering that many people meet their partners at work, how should one interpret an unwanted request for a date? Accepting or rejecting potential suitors is a part of courtship, so does a request from an undesired person constitute sexual harassment, when the same request from a desirable person does not? The former sometimes may be defined as unwanted sexual attention and treated as an instance of sexual harassment. Various potential problem areas in incidence studies are summarised in Table 3-3 below.

Table 3-3 *Methodological shortcomings in incidence studies*

Issue	Resulting problem
Each survey employs its own definition of sexual harassment	Results of these surveys cannot be integrated
Sexual harassment behaviours classified into arbitrary categories	Results in repetition, redundancy, omissions and confounding information
Use of unclear terms	Questions may be interpreted in different ways by respondents
Questionnaires consist of 'lists' of behaviours	They defines these behaviours as sexual harassment irrespective of what the respondent feels. This is inappropriate, except when the behaviour is so serious that the recipient's perception is irrelevant (such as assault)
Surveys employ different sampling techniques	Surveys of convenience may result in inflated incidence figures as only those people believed to be at risk are surveyed
Surveys may be gender or politically biased	Some surveys exclude the possibility of men being harassed, or assume that only those with formal power are capable of sexual harassment
Questionnaires are not piloted for reliability or validity	Some questionnaires are so poorly constructed, perhaps by containing incoherent or inconsistent questions, that one can only conclude they were 'thrown together' rather than being constructed. Internal company surveys, often created by people with no formal training in questionnaire design, are prime examples of questionnaires that clearly require testing for reliability and validity

One final issue concerning the existing incidence data is that most of the figures currently available are from the US. There have been a handful of studies carried out in the UK, such as the Leeds Trade Union survey (1983), but such studies are so varied in scope that they rarely add any new information to our understanding of sexual harassment. To date, there have been only a handful of incidence studies in Australia. One such study was undertaken as part of a larger study of technological experiences of bank employees in the mid–1980s. The authors, Soutar, Savery and Dufty (1987), asked members of the Australian Bank Employees Union in Western Australia, about their experiences of sexual harassment in the workplace. Over 300 women employees participated in the study. The main findings of the study are shown below in Table 3-4.

Table 3-4 *Sexual harassment in Western Australian banks*

Harassment situation	% experiencing behaviour several times	% experiencing behaviour once or twice
Made comments about you personally, in terms of your body, appearance, etc	23.1	42.5
Told jokes or had conversations about women which you found offensive	22.7	41.4
Made unwanted reference to your sex and personal life	12.9	27.5
Expressed a sexual interest in you which was unwanted	5.2	21.0
Verbally demanded or suggested an undesired sexual relationship, but taken no physical action	4.5	8.1
Molested you physically	3.2	12.6
Tried to force you into having unwanted sexual intercourse	1.0	2.3

Source: from Soutar, Savery and Dufty (1987).

The data also showed that only 20 per cent of the subjects had never experienced sexual harassment and that over 40 per cent had experienced three or more different forms of harassment. Interestingly, in a large number of cases the victims either laughed the situation off (about 46 per cent of subjects) or took no further action (about 32 per cent of subjects). Only 2.8 per cent complained to their manager, 2 per cent complained to a supervisor and 0.4 per cent made a formal complaint to the union. Such figures help to explain why supervisors and managers can erroneously believe that sexual harassment is not present in their workplace.

Assessing the incidence of sexual harassment with a questionnaire

Conducting a survey to assess the incidence of sexual harassment, either in a specific workforce population, or across the entire workforce, is clearly not straight-forward. Most surveys have suffered from either political biases or methodological shortcomings that undermine confidence in any findings. In the following sections we discuss how one might go about developing a questionnaire to assess incidence. The ideas presented here draw heavily on the authors' work in the development of an inventory—the Sexual Harassment in the Workplace Inventory (SHWI) in Appendix I—to measure the incidence of sexual harassment in the Australian work-place. In trying to develop a questionnaire to assess the incidence of sexual harassment a number of issues must be addressed.

The survey must reflect the legal definition of sexual harassment

Definitions of sexual harassment vary by state and country. For a survey to have any form of validity from a legal point of view, it must adhere to the requirements of the relevant laws. For example, most laws on sexual harassment make it possible for both men and women to be victims.

The survey must reflect each organisation's interpretation of sexual harassment

Many companies have adopted their own policies concerning sexual harassment. This will usually include a definition of sexual harassment, which in some cases is more stringent than that put forward in government legislation.

The survey must assess the full range of potential forms of sexual harassment

One of the most consistent failures of surveys is that they restrict the possible range of behaviours which might be classified as sexual harassment. Many instances of sexual harassment will be missed if questionnaire items are confined to a narrow set of behaviours. Further, if inappropriate assumptions are made (for example, specifying that abusers must be in a position of formal power over the victim) then this too will serve to produce unreliable statistics.

The questions must establish the context in which behaviours occur

As suggested earlier, including a survey item concerning sexual jokes (such as 'Does anyone in your workplace tell sexual jokes?'), does not allow us to infer that by endorsing this item that a person has experienced sexual harassment. Sexual harassment involves unwanted sexual behaviour and consequently questions on this topic must establish the relevant context that allow a behaviour to be defined as sexual harassment.

The questions must be unambiguous

The wording of the questions must be precise enough to ensure that respondents will respond consistently. The use of ambiguous terms can ensure that respondents will interpret questions subjectively. Questions should be phrased in behavioural terms, as in 'Have you ever...?', and not ask the respondent to infer the intentions of the other person.

Studies should sample the entire workforce

It is commonplace for organisations to carry out surveys by asking the opinions of managers or personnel directors. While data gathered from these people can often be informative, in this particular instance it is almost certain to produce only unreliable and spurious information. Many managers refuse to even consider the possibility of sexual harassment occurring in their organisations, and personnel directors will often base their answers on spurious data such as formal grievances.

The questions should avoid using the words 'sexual harassment'

The words 'sexual harassment' can be open to many different interpretations. It is strongly recommended that surveys should avoid using this term (even on the survey title) as it may influence responses (note that the SHWI does not feature these words). A person may freely admit they experienced unwanted sexual attention such as leering and obscene gestures, but decline to label it as sexual harassment. If it is considered necessary to explicitly ask about 'sexual harassment', then such questions should be positioned at the end of the survey or interview, depending on the format in which data is to be collected.

Finally, it is also worth considering that assessing incidence may include factors such as the frequency of occurrence, duration, relationships to the harasser and a host of other possible factors that may be shaped by the organisation's requirements.

Classifying types of sexual harassment

There have been a number of attempts to define the various forms that sexual harassment might take. Both Till and Fitzgerald (discussed earlier in this chapter) offered five distinct categories of sexual harassment. However, neither study is entirely satisfactory—they both fail to distinguish between some forms of harassment through the creation of overlapping categories. For example, Till's categorisation does not make a clear distinction between verbal requests and verbal remarks, making it possible for observers to classify a single behaviour differently. The authors' attempts to use Till's classification scheme with a class of postgraduate psychology students highlighted such problems, with the students unable to agree on how to classify a series of cases. In particular, there appears to be no obvious category for classifying sexual looks (such as *leering*) and there was some ambiguity over the distinction between verbal requests and verbal statements.

In order to clarify the various forms of sexual harassment, we present the following categorisation scheme, which was used in the development of the SHWI. The original premise is that sexual harassment behaviours can be classified across several dimensions.

Direct and indirect behaviours

First, a distinction is made between behaviours that are targeted at a particular person (direct) and those that are not directed at any one person in particular (indirect). On occasions there may be a blurring between these categories, but in most cases this distinction is easily made. If the behaviour is directed to an individual (such as comments to that person or leaving offensive material in that person's desk) then it is clear that the harasser(s) has a specific target in mind. However, behaviours such as the display of pornographic calendars in public areas where a number of workers may see them, are seen as indirect. Obviously, on some occasions it is possible that seemingly indirect behaviours (such as pin-ups) are targeted at a particular person, but it would be very difficult for an independent observer to infer this. Generally, indirect harassment is seen as contributing to a 'hostile working environment'.

Rewards and punishments

The second distinction to make is whether there is any outcome tied to the occurrence of a behaviour. If a supervisor threatens a worker with dismissal (or offers a reward for compliance with sexual requests) then this type of behaviour is known as *quid pro quo*. In most countries a legal distinction is made between behaviours that carry promises of rewards or sanctions and those that do not. Offering rewards or punishments is typically the prerogative of supervisors or employers, that is, where the harasser is in a superior position to the victim. Such behaviours represent a misuse of organisational power that are widely perceived as the most clear-cut instances of sexual harassment. *Quid pro quo* harassment must, by practical necessity, be a form of direct sexual harassment.

It is not difficult to provide examples of *quid pro quo* harassment. Invariably a verbal statement, whether written or spoken, coercion and bribery involve the harasser telling or suggesting to the victim to do or participate in something of a sexual nature for a reward or, if refused, with consequent punishment. If taken literally, *quid pro quo* may also involve the offer of a reward of a sexual kind in exchange for a benefit (usually work-related) to the harasser. The latter example, reportedly rare, but always newsworthy, can be exemplified by the female who 'gets ahead' in an organisation by offering sexual favours. For feminists, this does not constitute sexual harassment, as it does not fit the model of the female oppressed by a man in a position of power, and also because usually she is not in a position to take reprisals if he refuses her advances. However, from a purely definitional and legal perspective this exchange should be seen as sexual harassment because it involves sex, coercion or bribery and the consequences are irrelevant.

Form of behaviour

This type of classification refers to the form the harassment takes—in other words, how it is expressed. At the simplest level, there might be verbal comments or remarks, verbal requests (where some behaviour or reaction is required), non-verbal displays (for example, gestures such as leering or ogling, and breathing down the phone) and physical behaviours (such as overt touching, brushing, patting, pinching and grabbing, through to sexual assault and rape).

Taking into account the possible combinations of these dimensions we arrived at the following scheme (see Table 3-5 below). The examples given do not address the full range of behaviours that might fall within each category.

Table 3-5 *Categories of sexual harassment*

Types of sexual harassment	Possible examples
Direct sexual harassment	
Hostile environment	
1. Verbal requests (orally or in writing)	Annette regularly asks David, a married colleague, to come her house (alone) for dinner, or to go to the cinema or concerts together
2. Verbal remarks (orally or in writing)	Hanif frequently makes comments about Christine's appearance. He describes her as 'elegant but not quite sexy' and offers advice on how to 'dress to kill'
3. Non-verbal displays and behaviours	Malcolm works in a warehouse and regularly pretends to masturbate in front of the female staff
4. Physical behaviours	Marguerite and Ted are colleagues in a small office. She frequently brushes past him, touches him on the hand, pats his buttocks and strokes his hair

Types of sexual harassment   Possible examples

Quid pro quo

1. Coercion	The boss of a small firm is homosexual and warns his employees that unless they accompany him to a gay club every Friday night he will fire them
2. Bribery	A supervisor makes remarks to female subordinates that he could give them more interesting work 'if they were nice to him'

Indirect sexual harassment

Hostile environment

1. Verbal remarks	Denise is the head of a small firm and constantly refers to men as 'useless pricks' and 'lazy bastards'
2. Non-verbal displays	The workers at a computer firm have pornographic calendars on their walls

The prevalent nature of sexual harassment

Even though studies have used different definitions and different approaches to researching sexual harassment, they consistently show that workers may regularly experience a variety of forms of unwanted sexual attention in the workplace. It is hard to put an accurate figure on how many people are harassed, yet the data suggest that a majority of workers, in particular women, are likely to encounter sexual harassment in some form at some stage of their careers.

Studies have also shown that management and personnel officers are typically unaware of harassment in their own workplaces. This may occur for a variety of reasons—workers may be reluctant to report instances of harassment, perhaps fearing the consequences or possibly deciding that they have misinterpreted an innocent (or plain clumsy) behaviour. It is also the case that, until recently, many companies have lacked any appropriate channels for reporting such grievances. Workers may be expected to take grievances to unsympathetic supervisors, who may even be the harassers. This was illustrated by one victim of sexual harassment the authors interviewed, who told us how she was delighted to learn that her employers were introducing sexual harassment officers, to whom victims could report. As a previous victim of harassment, she understood the need for such a person in her workplace. However, in a situation that almost defies belief, she found that her newly appointed 'sexual harassment officer' was a supervisor who had previously sexually harassed her!

Incidence studies are a useful way of finding out the extent to which harassment is an issue in a given workforce, but the lack of an agreed survey methodology and the poor choice of survey items may make them invalid. Surveys are a potentially valuable tool, provided they are carried out using a representative sample of workers and an appropriate questionnaire structure.

Any organisation seriously committed to eliminating sexual harassment in the workplace must carry out incidence studies, both prior to, and after, any interventions to reduce sexual harassment have been introduced. Without this simple set of 'before and after' figures it is impossible to gauge the effectiveness of training programmes or other interventions. After all, one cannot claim to have eradicated or reduced a problem if it is unclear whether the problem was present in the first place.

part two

Causes and consequences for workers and organisations

chapter four

Why does sexual harassment occur?

The objectives of this chapter are:
*to examine the concept of 'power' and how it is related to
    sexual harassment*
*to identify and explore six major reasons why sexual harassment
    may occur.*

Why would someone sexually harass another person? Many writers have tried to *infer* single motives to account for the diverse range of behaviours that constitute sexual harassment, but this often tells us more about the predispositions of the authors, than it does about the problem itself. Given that sexual harassment may include behaviours ranging from personal comments to rape (depending on the definition used), a satisfactory explanation is unlikely to be forthcoming. Many of the suggested explanations rely on untestable assumptions and therefore the debate shows little sign of easy resolution. Nevertheless, as we will discuss in this chapter, researchers have developed some interesting hypotheses about the causes of sexual harassment, some of which have received support.

In this chapter we identify several possible motives for sexual harassment. Each of these motives shares one common factor, namely the concept of *power*. Power can take many forms, but without some form of power of the harasser over the harassed, sexual harassment is unlikely to occur. Even a subordinate who harasses a supervisor invokes a form of power. Given the significance of power to an understanding of why sexual harassment occurs, we begin by outlining some of the most important forms of power.

Box 4-1 *Why does sexual harassment occur?*

Why do you think sexual harassment occurs? Before reading this chapter write down the main reasons why you think someone would want to harass another person. If you know of any cases of sexual harassment, try to infer why the harasser chose to behave in that way.

What is power?

In their discussion of the role of power in organisations, psychologists Jeannette Cleveland and Melinda Kerst (1993) summarise what is known about the concept of power. They suggest that power entails the capability of one person to overcome resistance in achieving a desired objective or results. Power can stem from *societal, organisational, interpersonal or individual* factors (see Table 4-1) and can be used to further *legitimate* or *illegitimate* goals.

In many analyses of why sexual harassment occurs, the concepts of sex and power are seen as core components. For example, Donna Stringer and her colleagues argue that there are two main motivations to harass:

- to obtain sexual activity (the use of power to obtain sex)
- to abuse or increase one's power (the use of sex to obtain/maintain power).

These two motives are not mutually exclusive.

Note that in order to harass another person, the harasser needs some form of power, but having power does not inevitably mean that a person will harass others. This point is seemingly self-evident, but in some feminist discussions of this topic this concept is all too easily ignored, and the possession of power is seen as an inevitable invitation to harass. Although many men do harass and it is a prevalent problem, it is a mistake to believe that all men will harass. To argue otherwise exonerates individual organisations from their responsibility in dealing with sexual harassment, since it becomes an issue that could only be tackled societally.

Table 4-1 *Sources of power in organisations*

Societal power	In every society some groups of people have more power over others. It is generally accepted that in Western societies men have more power over women.
Organisational power	Some individuals have power based on their position in organisational hierarchies.
Interpersonal power	Certain personal attributes may give some individuals more power. Examples are intelligence and aptitude.
Situational power	Circumstances may arise where an individual is temporarily in a position of power over another, perhaps by being central to controlling the distribution of information.
Perceived power	Some people appear to others as being powerful or more powerful than they actually are. This perception in itself may be a source of power for these people.

The exercise of power

Possessing power over another person is not necessarily related to formal organisational power. As described below, this is but one of the ways in which the exercise of power can be manifest in the workplace.

Sexual harassment by superiors

Being in a position of formal power allows the harasser more latitude (the capability) for harassment and more ways in which to pursue it. A supervisor has not only greater authority and influence but also influences the climate of the workplace—whether a sexually loaded or sexist or homophobic atmosphere is accepted. They set behavioural examples; they are role models. People in a position of authority have the say in the working lives (promotions, evaluations) of the subordinates. *Quid pro quo* sexual harassment invariably involves a superior because only a superior is in a position to offer rewards or punishment in exchange for sexual activity.

Traditionally this scenario has involved a man harassing a woman, because it is more common to find men in positions of formal power and also because of the fact that most harassers are male. In principle, they can employ all forms and types of sexual harassment (*quid pro quo*, hostile environment, verbal, non-verbal and physical forms) as described in Chapter 3. Although studies have shown that most of the superior–subordinate harassment is initiated by men, little is known about the harassment perpetrated by a woman in a position of formal power over her subordinates. There is also little known about male–male superior to subordinate harassment. In this case, the superior may have a sexual motive (wanting a homosexual relationship) or may use sexual references to demean or humiliate the subordinate, for example, if the subordinate is homosexual and the superior is not. At least one case has been recorded in which a female superior sexually harassed a female subordinate, even though neither was homosexual. In this case, the superior made constant references to the subordinate's past sexual history and physical appearance (for example, she would rub her own breasts and make reference to them in front of the subordinate). In this particular case the motive appears to have been intimidatory bullying, the sexual aspect being present because it is a salient and effective ploy through which to embarrass another person.

Sexual harassment by co-workers

The original view of sexual harassment conceptualised a formal power differential between the parties. However, most of the sexual harassment reported in the major surveys reviewed in Chapter 3, confirm that co-worker harassment is the most prevalent. Here it is more difficult to ascertain where the power sources lie, or whether power (as it is conventionally interpreted) plays any role at all. In reviewing this type of harassment, Cleveland and Kerst remind us that there can be power differences through informal networks, level of support and decision-making on the part of the supervisor. Co-workers cannot usually engage in *quid pro quo* harassment because they do not have the resources to punish or reward for sexual relations. They can however, contribute to a hostile working environment—in particular, if the supervisor in charge has a non-caring attitude or sets the wrong example. Analyses of co-workers harassment lend support to the view that even when men and women occupy the same formal position, often she does not have the same level of authority or influence (in other words, the woman does not have perceived power), particularly if the supervisor of both parties gives the man more power.

Although not usually in a position to punish or reward, co-workers can provide or withhold support and co-operation. In an environment which is male-dominated, for example, a woman can be seen as a threat or an outsider. In this case, sexual harassment can be used to isolate her and prevent her from joining the peer-support network. This can have negative consequences for the person harassed and can affect the quality of their work and job satisfaction. An analysis of the harassment of women by men colleagues in male dominated environments and/or professions, appears to support this contention. Little is known however about the plight of men in female dominated settings in particular, as many of the settings that have been studied (with a majority of women and few men) usually involve male superiors working with a larger number of women subordinates.

Sexual harassment by subordinates

For those who adhere to the view that sexual harassment can only be initiated by persons in positions of formal power, the notion of subordinates harassing will sound alien. However, as we have described above, it is possible for any person to make another feel harassed, whether there is a legal case or not.

This type of harassment is sometimes called *contrapower harassment* and it is not infrequent in university settings, particularly from male students to female academic staff. Here, the goal of the harasser appears to be that of devaluing the woman and her power by reminding her of her sexual or gender stereotype. As is the case with co-worker harassment, the goal of the harasser is to minimise the power between himself and the target or to seek to gain power.

Sexual hassle is a form of contrapower harassment when the harasser is a woman and the target a man. Her goal and motives may be exactly the same as those of a male subordinate but most of what is known about it derives from anecdotal evidence and little is known about its prevalence and how it is manifested. A number of feminist writers are of the view that the existence of sexual hassle is a male myth and constitutes an attack on the seriousness of women's plight by suggesting that only women have the power to use their sexuality to their advantage. Although sexual hassle may not represent a structural/societal phenomenon (abuse of one group over another), its existence is nevertheless testimony that unwanted and persistent sexual pestering is indeed, psychologically speaking, sexual harassment.

Motives for sexual harassment

In the following sections we identify the most important motives for sexual harassment. Unfortunately, sexual harassment is often oversimplified and mistakenly conceptualised as either a form of sex discrimination, or as 'attraction gone wrong'. This simplistic approach only serves to hinder an understanding of the problem. There is no single explanation that 'works' across all situations. Further, it is also possible that harassers may have multiple reasons for sexually harassing another person.

Sexual discrimination

Discrimination is usually at the core of sexual harassment, particularly with men discriminating against women in the workplace. This premise is the basis of legislation in many countries where sexual harassment is a form of sex discrimination, that is, something that would not happen to a person if it were not for their sex.

Discrimination can take many forms, where one societal group discriminates against a less powerful minority. Obvious examples are discrimination against homosexuals and racial discrimination. Sexual discrimination is often seen as stemming from the existence of a patriarchal society in which men and women are socialised to play specific roles. Society rewards men for aggression and dominance and women for passivity and acquiescence. According to this explanation, the harassed are women and the harassers are men, and all forms of sexual behaviour should serve the same purpose, namely to keep women in subordinate positions.

Although there is a strong intuitive rationale for this proposal, it fails to account for all instances of sexual harassment. Based on findings from the USMSPB study, Sandra Tangri and colleagues (1982) argued that this theory could not be wholly endorsed as it failed to explain why some men were sexually harassed. Further, findings that single women were more likely to be harassed than married women further undermines this proposal, since all women should be discriminated against equally. Additionally, not all men harass women.

While sexual discrimination is often a key motive in harassment, it is not the only reason. Countries that classify sexual harassment as an example of sexual discrimination (such as England and Australia) will inevitably find that the legislation is inadequate. This point was dramatically illustrated in a recent case in England, where a woman's complaint about a calendar displaying pictures of naked women was dismissed, because it was reasoned that a 'hypothetical man' might also have found the pictures offensive. Because sex was deemed irrelevant to the case, the issue of discrimination was not supported. Until sexual harassment is better understood, current sex discrimination laws may be ill-equipped to deal with situations such as this.

Sexual interest

Sexual harassment is often conceptualised as an 'attraction issue', or more specifically, that it is about attraction gone wrong. For example, men may argue that they are simply trying to establish relationships with female colleagues as part of their normal courting rituals, and that complaining about such behaviour reflects an inappropriate level of sensitivity from women who should be better equipped to cope with such advances. Essentially this shifts the burden of responsibility for dealing with sexual harassment onto the victim, where *their* lack of social skills are put at fault.

It has been hypothesised that 'attraction gone wrong' may occur because men's assertiveness makes it hard for them to control their sex drives. Men, it is argued, may have a higher sex drive than women, which explains why most victims are women. If this is the case, then sexual harassment is a result of biological factors and the most likely initiators of sexual behaviours would be men who are at the age of their peak sex-drive, regardless of their status within the organisation.

Another version of this model makes no reference to an unequal sex drive but stresses that an individual may be attracted to another and willing to express this attraction. It would therefore be expected that both men and women would be equally likely to initiate the behaviours and that their targets would be of similar ages and background, consistent with the findings of the literature on romance and courtship. This model also posits that there may be some men with tendencies to initiate social–sexual behaviours even when they are not reciprocated. This behaviour may not be ideal, but does not follow a systematic pattern and is not meant to offend or discriminate.

If we assume that sexual harassment is fundamentally an issue of attraction, then to a large extent we are trivialising the nature of the problem. If such behaviour is natural then it seems illogical to talk of punishing such behaviour since efforts to curtail these expressions would be futile.

Fortunately, it is relatively easy to discount attraction as a primary motive in most cases of sexual harassment. Whichever way the attraction notion is put forward, it raises assumptions that are not borne out by empirical findings. These findings include facts such as that the parties involved in cases of harassment are not typically of similar backgrounds and occupational status. Nor are they both unmarried and 'available'. Further, the recipients do not feel flattered by the attention they receive and the rewards and punishments attached to some advances are clearly not part of normal courtship rituals. Finally, workplace characteristics should have little relevance to these behaviours, but as we will see later in this chapter, they are clearly important.

Although it is possible that some cases of harassment are about attraction gone wrong, it is likely to be the case that such situations are relatively rare. Harassers do not behave in ways that would be typical of someone trying to establish a romantic relationship or friendship. If their motives were honourable then they would not attach conditions or threats to their requests for dates, they would (typically) be sympathetic to negative responses and they would focus their attention on one person at a time.

One final issue relating to the attraction motive is the widely cited finding that men tend to perceive women's friendly behaviour as sexual. This is based on a series of studies by US researcher, Antonia Abbey. Abbey (1982) found that if men and women were asked to watch other men and women engaging in everyday conversations, the male observers often inferred that the women were 'acting sexy' or 'flirtatious', even though their actual behaviour had been completely devoid of any such connotation. In contrast, women observers failed to see any sexual content in the exchanges. These findings have been taken to suggest that men misinterpret women's friendly behaviour as sexual attention. This might lend some support to the notion that men might pester women with uninvited requests for dates. However, an innocent misunderstanding is likely to be rectified by the woman's first refusal to go out on a date. If the man should persist in his requests or threaten reprisals in any way, then that behaviour would constitute sexual harassment. Although such explanations may have some relevance to a small number of cases of harassment, they are clearly irrelevant in cases involving offensive displays, comments and behaviour, or where some threat is involved.

Assertion of formal power

One of the most obvious ways in which power and sexual harassment are linked is in the notion that managers or supervisors harass subordinates as a way of asserting their power. That is, to establish their superiority, through the diminishing of another's power, may lie at the heart of why some people with power harass others. The motive then is power, not sex.

Most workplaces are organised around a hierarchical system (vertical stratification) that provides the opportunity for individuals with greater power within the organisation to behave towards subordinates as they see fit. This makes men the most likely perpetrators due to their higher status in most organisations. Subordinates, who are in most cases women, are left vulnerable to these advances because if they react against these behaviours their jobs may be jeopardised. In most instances, women cannot afford to lose their jobs, so that they are economically dependent and consequently vulnerable. The issue of unequal power distribution is central to this model. Following such premises, targets of harassment should be low in organisational power, whereas harassers should have a higher status within the organisation.

Despite the existence of differences in the power and prestige of positions held by men and women in organisations, the existing data do not support the formal power differential perspective. The finding that harassers are often not supervisors suggests that other mechanisms besides organisational power differences contribute to the occurrence of sexual harassment.

Organisational culture

Many studies have found that there are strong links between organisational culture and the existence of sexual harassment. Put simply, there are certain types of workplace culture in which sexual harassment can thrive, and others in which it becomes unlikely. The amount of interest in this particular explanation of harassment reflects the fact that organisational culture may be modifiable.

Kanter's tokenism

Researchers have identified a number of different ways in which organisational culture can influence sexual harassment. One of the earliest indications of a link came from the research by Rosabeth Moss Kanter (1977). Kanter was interested in the problems faced by women who occupied positions in predominantly male workforces. She argued that the culture of the dominant group predominates in any workplace and those that do not fall into this majority may be classed as 'tokens'. Tokens then stand out in the organisation because of their characteristics that distinguish them from the majority. For example, in an organisation where most engineers are men, a female engineer would stand out as a woman rather than as an engineer. Kanter also believed that, as groups reached numerical parity, tokenism would disappear, although each subgroup may create their own differentiations based on other structural or personal factors (like ability).

According to Kanter's analysis, problems are created for women when they become tokens in male-dominated groups. In a study of *Fortune 500* firms, Kanter found that in the presence of women, men highlighted what they could do as men in contrast to women. Compared to instances in which only men were present, there were more sexual innuendos and off-colour jokes. For Kanter these occurrences are ways of making clear the expected cultural rules under which women were to be allowed to interact with the group. Women, were not, nevertheless, supposed to behave in the way which is accepted for the male culture (such as telling dirty jokes or swearing).

One of the most interesting aspects of Kanter's work was her description of the ways in which token women would be classified within the workplace. She described four roles that could be adopted by token women: mother, seductress, pet and iron maiden. The 'mother' adopted the nurturing maternal role. She would listen to male peer group problems and even take on their domestic chores. She retained her power provided she was accepting and uncritical of male behaviour, offering no competition in the public sphere. The 'seductress' was cast as a sex object and aroused sexual competition if she shared her affections or sexual jealousy if she formed an alliance with one man. The 'pet' was adopted as a group mascot who admired and encouraged male prowess. Displays of competence were complimented for their rarity, or on other task irrelevant grounds. This encouraged self-effacing, girlish responses from the women, which prevented them from demonstrating their own power or competence. The 'iron maiden' refused to adopt any of the other three roles by insisting on her rights. She was stereotyped as tough and was forced into a militant stance.

Although it is possible to find examples where women have adopted such roles, Kanter's work has been criticised for the fact that her ideas on minorities only seem to apply to women. That is, when men are in a minority in the workplace then they do not seem to suffer from a comparable form of tokenism.

Gutek's sex-role spillover

Kanter's work was subsequently expanded by Barbara Gutek (1985) when she developed her concepts of *sex-role spillover*. Gutek suggested that when an occupation is dominated by people of either sex, the sex-role of the dominant gender (male or female) will spill over into the work-role expectations. For example, those occupations that are dominated by women will, according to this explanation, become sexualised and the sex role of the women more pronounced. A case in point would be that of nurses, airline stewards, waitresses and secretaries. It is common for these jobs to become sexualised (obvious examples include caricatures of these women as sex objects) which is also reflected in the way some of these women are supposed to dress, look and act. Women in these positions are seen as women first and as workers second.

According to Gutek, as more women join the labour force, one would expect a reduction in sex-role spillover. She believes that sex ratios at work operate at three different levels: occupations have sex ratios (for example, most plumbers are men, most airline stewards are women); jobs have sex ratios, which means that even if a woman's occupation is non-traditional she could still be working in a female dominated environment (for example, an engineering firm which employs mainly female engineers); and work-role sets. *Work-role set* is a concept used to delineate people with whom one is directly associated at work, usually through work flow. The amount of time one spends at work with the opposite sex is another factor affecting people's behaviour and experiences at work.

These three types of sex ratio can be ordered in terms of immediacy and impact on day-to-day experiences at work and would affect workers in the following way (Gutek's analysis focuses on the female sex-role spillover exclusively). Gutek believes that women whose occupations are non-traditional will stand out as women because their sex role is incongruent with their work role (for example, an army officer). They are seen as *women* in jobs. On the other side of the spectrum, women employed in traditional occupations are seen as conforming to sex-role expectations. Because a female job is dominated by one sex, the job itself takes on aspects of the sex role (for example, nurses). Different traditional female jobs emphasise different aspects of the female sex role. The traditionally employed woman is typecast because of her occupation. She may not notice it because other women might also be treated in the same way.

Interestingly, Gutek found that women in integrated jobs are less likely than working women in general to report problems of sexual behaviour at work. Male and female roles seem to be downplayed in this kind of environment. It is possible that integrated work environments contain less stereotyped sex-role behaviour but also exhibit less defensiveness about male–female interaction. Although many aspects of gender roles can carry over to work, the sex object aspect is the most relevant to the topic of sex at work. Being a sex object is one aspect of the female sex role, but it is not clear whether a comparable sexual aspect applies to men. In any event, the carryover of the sexual aspects of sex roles into the workplace is likely to be related to sexuality at work.

Pryor's person and situation

One limitation of both Kanter and Gutek's arguments is that even when the workplace is skewed in favour of one sex, it is not inevitable that those in the majority will act in a harassing manner. According to psychologist John Pryor (1993), there are situational factors that, when combined with personal factors, may result in sexual harassment. Situational factors include the sexualisation of the work environment, as Gutek had suggested, and the strength of local norms. Norms created by management may contribute to the atmosphere or culture of the workplace and have a bearing upon the occurrence of discrimination and harassment. Management sets the rules and the norms of a workplace, which determine not only the occurrence of sexual harassment but of reactions to it. Sexual harassment will be more prevalent in a workplace more tolerant of sexual harassment.

Personal factors would include personal or psychological characteristics, such as the age or marital status of the harasser and personal endorsement of sexual (exploitative) behaviours. Pryor believes that certain men may be more prone to sexually harass and created a measure of what he called 'Likelihood to Sexually Harass' (LSH). This scale, described in detail in Chapter 5, focuses exclusively on extreme forms of harassment, most specifically *quid pro quo*. The LSH presents men with ten situations in which they control rewards or punishments to an attractive woman. Men then are asked to rate their likelihood of 'sexually exploiting women'. Their responses are taken as an indication of the proclivity to sexually harass. Pryor believes that men who are more prone to sexually harass will harass in circumstances where the situational factors or social norms permit it.

The person/situation explanation can be a practical framework for further investigation into sexual harassment in organisations. Regarding 'person' factors, the LSH, or other psychological profile measures, can be used to assess the readiness or proclivity to engage in sexually exploitative actions. Research studies have shown that the impact of situational norms can be key to the expression of sexual harassment proclivities. The presence of a 'harassing role model' enhanced the chances that a man with a high LSH would commit harassment.

Taken together, the work of these researchers suggests that the organisational culture appears to influence the extent to which sexual harassment is present in the workplace. This is a particularly important finding, as workplace cultures may be amenable to change.

Personal motives

Sexual harassment may be used for personal motives. For example, it may be used to cause distress to an individual the harasser does not like. It may be that a harasser does not dislike women as a whole, but does dislike one particular woman. Here then, harassment is a form of bullying. The reason that the harassment is sexual is simply because sex is a highly salient characteristic and can be used relatively easily to cause offence. For many people discussions of sexual matters are highly personal and may cause embarrassment when raised in public. The harasser is aware of this and tries to embarrass the target of their dislike by, for example, asking embarrassing questions in public.

It is of course also possible that sexual harassment reflects some degree of personal pathology on the part of the harasser. This may include undergoing some form of personal crisis in which their sexuality is threatened, to which they respond by over-asserting their sexuality. It is also possible that the behaviour reflects a genuine deviance, perhaps based on alcohol abuse. In such cases the harasser is likely to target a number of other workers and to persist in such behaviours even when staff leave and replacements arrive.

Sex to obtain power

While power may be used to obtain sex, it is also possible that sex can be used to obtain power. This may take two forms. First, sexual hassle, which occurs when a person uses sex to obtain rewards. For example, a female worker might befriend a male colleague, or flirt with him, as part of a strategy to win his favour and subsequently some form of reward, such as being recommended for promotion. Almost always, the harasser will have less formal power than the person being harassed. In some feminist analyses this form of harassment is dismissed since it is rare, and also because it is argued that the male superior still holds power over the female and should be able to stop the harassment if desired.

Second, Elizabeth Grauerholz (1989) suggests that there is contrapower harassment, where a subordinate uses sex to cause distress to a superior. The most common example here is that of students who harass lecturers by leaving suggestive notes under their doors, or obscene graffiti on desks and walls. In such cases the student has a form of situational power (they remain anonymous) and the lecturer is powerless to act against that person.

Inferring intention in the behaviour of others

At the start of this chapter you were asked to write down the main reasons why you thought harassment occurs. Most people cite the concept of power in some way, either seeing harassment as the use of power to obtain sex, or sex to obtain power (for example, discrimination). All too often it has been assumed that one single explanation accounts for all sexual harassment. Unfortunately, proponents of such views often reduce the problem into simplistic terms that fail to recognise the diverse range of behaviours that can constitute sexual harassment.

Best-selling author Katie Roiphe (1994) argues that victims of sexual harassment should develop their social skills and thereby fend off the unwanted advances of lecherous males. In this conception, sexual harassment is reduced to a form of misdirected attention that can be remedied by clearly stating to the offenders that their behaviour is not welcome. One successful strategy she describes is that of a college student who tipped a glass of milk over her aggressor. While there may be occasions when this is a suitable strategy, these occasions are not likely to be very common or very effective. By viewing sexual harassment in such simplistic terms the problem is reduced to one of bad manners or poor social skills.

As we have discussed, there are a wide variety of motives for sexual harassment. However, inferring the motives of a particular harasser can be extremely difficult. It may be that harassers have more than one reason for harassing and trying to decide why an individual has harassed another may be an impossibility.

chapter five

Who are the harassers?

The objectives of this chapter are:
to look at the personality and behavioural characteristics of
male harassers
to examine the possibility of identifying potential harassers

Incidence studies of sexual harassment have generally provided only a sketchy picture of those most likely to experience sexual harassment (see Chapter 3). Not surprisingly then, our understanding of those who perpetrate acts of sexual harassment is even less clear-cut. This is largely because we tend to derive our information about who the harassers are from the accounts of the harassed, which may be biased. For example, perhaps those who are harassed are more likely to report certain types of harasser (such as managers) because they anticipate that accusations against other workers (such as colleagues or clients) might be less credible. A further problem is that harassers are not likely to readily volunteer their names for the purposes of research studies, although there are a small number who will do so, as will be discussed later in the chapter.

This chapter explores issues such as 'who are the harassers and what makes them harass?'. We concentrate here on those who engage in the most overtly sexual forms of sexual harassment, as opposed to those who conduct gender based or misogynistic forms of harassment. Such an analysis raises a number of important questions for human resources practitioners. Most significantly, is it possible to identify potential harassers and to then screen out such individuals as part of the personnel selection process? The attraction of this idea is simple: it might be possible to eradicate (or substantially reduce) sexual harassment by the use of questionnaires or structured interviews. We begin our examination of harassers by focusing on research conducted in university settings, because direct examination of workplace harassers has been scarce.

The lecherous professor

Most of us have heard stories of infatuated young female students falling for the charms of their wise, worldly and commanding professors. This was the underlying topic in the film *Gross Misconduct*, set in a Melbourne-based university, where a professor is accused of raping a student with whom he has had a brief affair. However, for the most part, these relationships are depicted as consensual and non-exploitative, such as in the film of *The Pelican Brief*, where Julia Roberts is dating her professor. Such accounts, often romanticised, typically ignore that for the most part, consensual relationships in such situations are rare, and that exploitation and coercion of a sexual nature are more prevalent. As we saw in Chapter 2, Australian universities rarely prohibit sexual relationships between staff and students.

We know very little about why some instructors or lecturers sexually harass their students. Given the sensitivity of the topic and the controversy surrounding it, it would be almost impossible to ask 'harassers' what they do, and why they do it, directly. As Sue Rosenberg Zalk says, those who sexually harass are reticent to volunteer to participate in studies, for who would not only recognise their behaviour as harassment and admit to being a harasser but also volunteer to aid researchers?

As with the situation in the workplace, the lecturer–harasser does not call himself a harasser or his actions harassing. However, lecturers know they hold societal, formal and situational power (see Chapter 4). Analysts of sexual harassment in academia, such as Donna Benson and Gregg Thomson (1982), believe it is the combination of these sources of power, coupled with long-entrenched misogyny, that give rise to sexual harassment on campus.

In 1984 American writers Billie Wright Dziech and Linda Weiner published *The Lecherous Professor: Sexual Harassment on Campus*, a landmark text on the topic of sexual harassment in higher education. In a compelling and thorough chapter, filled with careful observations and insight of life on campus ('A Portrait of the Artist'), they suggest that there are two types of harasser—the public harasser and the private harasser. The public harasser behaves in an informal fashion and is typically a young and friendly lecturer. He likes to spend most of his time with students, be it in his office, at the student union or bars. He is described by these authors as someone articulate, funny, glib and sarcastic. His behaviour is seldom coercive, but rather, seductive and overly friendly.

The private harasser is at the opposite pole. This man represents the typical academic stereotype. He is a formal and conservative dresser. He has a formal demeanour and manner; he may even appear intimidating as a figure of authority whom one has to obey and respect. This harasser would use his formal authority to coerce a student into a sexual relationship. He shields himself in the sanctuary of his office, where his actions may spell straightforward coercion in the vein of 'If you are nice to me, I'll give you a good grade, but if not, you may be in trouble'. As well as suggesting the existence of two types of harasser, the authors believe that the harassers adopt certain roles when dealing with female students. Their analysis of these roles is interesting and helps us to understand the various ways in which sexual harassment can be manifested. These roles are summarised in Table 5-1.

Table 5-1 *The roles adopted by harassers in academia*

1. The Counsellor–Helper

This harasser outwardly behaves like a nurturer or caretaker. He encourages the student to trust and confide in him and once is aware of her vulnerabilities he chooses 'his line'. For example, a professor who asks a student to describe how she had been rejected by her boyfriend and then says that he would never behave in 'that way'. In addition, the Counsellor–Helper may act as a go-between in his female students' relationships, thus deriving vicarious sexual pleasure, or as an ombudsman described it, 'pimping'.

2. The Confidante

This harasser also acts like the student's friend. He shares personal information and invites confidences from the student. He also offers his own confidences starting a web of 'trust' in which the student becomes increasingly involved, feeling increasingly indebted and finds almost impossible to break free from.

3. The Intellectual Seducer

Sometimes referred to as 'mind fucking' or 'intellectual intercourse'. This harasser gains personal information about his students while blinding them with his knowledge of academic topics. He encourages confidences, which may be related to his course topic. For example, a literature professor discussing erotic fantasy in literature, may lead his students to relate their fantasies to him. A variation on the theme is the harasser who uses his knowledge to seduce women.

4. The Opportunist

This is the harasser who takes advantage of their situational power. The professor who uses physical proximity to his advantage, such as helping an assistant in a lab session. He also uses opportunities in other settings which are not as formal and restricting, such as field trips or conferences, to try to take advantage of his students.

5. The Power Broker

Typified by the private harasser, this man has the power to control grades, references and job opportunities. He holds the stakes and may not only coerce the students into doing something for a grade, but also, and worse in some respects, bribe the student subtly with promises of help. A clear case of rewards and punishments, as described in Chapter 3.

Source: adapted from Dziech and Weiner's *The Lecherous Professor* (1990).

Dziech and Weiner also discuss the demographic and attitudinal characteristics of these men and the life events which may have led to their harassing behaviour. They paint a convincing picture of the psychology of the harasser, that fits many a description of student experiences. This analysis, however, is superficial and it is insufficient for anyone to conclude that there are in-depth differences between those who harass and those who do not. Dziech and Weiner, as well as

Zalk, state that perhaps men who choose the academic world as a profession do so because they have failed in other domains during adolescence: attractiveness to the opposite sex, popularity and athleticism. These former 'failures' may prompt the men to choose an environment where they can 'cure' their self-doubt, their inadequacies about their sexuality, while enhancing their ego and enjoying the power that an academic profession bestows upon them. Although some may find such an argument credible, it ignores the obvious problem that similar types of harassment are seen across all types of occupations and settings. This undermines the notion that there may be patterns of career preferences which appeal to harassers.

Harassers in the workplace

The two USMSPB studies (see Chapter 3) probably provide the best data for identifying harassers in the workplace. The study attempted to determine whether harassers tended to have specific positions within organisations, whether harassers of men and women differed markedly, as well as other data on patterns of harassment, such as whether harassment was confined to isolated incidents or part of a systematic pattern. Table 5-2 summarises the data on the relative positions of harassers. Although the general patterns for male and female workers are similar, there are some interesting differences. For example, females were more likely to be harassed by higher level supervisors (though not immediate supervisors) than men, while men were more likely to be harassed by subordinates.

Overall, the research data, from both the USMSPB studies and that of Gutek, suggest that the typical harasser is a white, male co-worker. He is also likely to be married and older than the target of his harassment. Further, harassment is not confined to isolated events. Instead harassers generally show a pattern of harassment over prolonged time periods, often against multiple targets. When questioned about his actions, he will deny that he is a harasser (this is not surprising) and that his motives and actions have been misunderstood and blown out of proportion. The accuser may well be labelled as a troublemaker.

Table 5-2 *Organisational level of harassers, USMSPB (1987 study)*

Source of harassment	% of victims claiming their harassers were at the organisational level shown	
	Female	*Male*
Immediate supervisor	12	12
Higher level supervisor	19	10
Co-worker	41	47
Subordinate	2	10
Other employees	37	40
Other or unknown	10	10

This profile strongly refutes the notion that harassment is the result of disputes between individuals. The major limitation of the demographic information on harassers is obvious. In describing the average harasser as a white male co-worker, one is also describing the 'average worker'. Gutek argues that the characteristics of the male harassers in her study bore no differences to those of the average male worker. To illustrate this point, she says that of the men in her sample, 53 per cent were 36 years of age or older and 68 per cent of them were married. Amongst the harassers, 49 per cent were 40 or over and 65 per cent were married. It appears that on the basis of demographic data alone, it is not possible to form a portrait of a typical harasser.

It seems that the data do not provide any great insights that would allow organisations to target either selection or training to eliminate sexual harassment. Louise Fitzgerald and Lauren Weitzman (1988) note that although this may be an accurate portrait, the information that comes from women's accounts only represents those cases that had the greatest effect on them. It is possible that the harassment described represents the extreme, obvious forms and that there are many more varieties of harassers.

The arguments for and against the existence of a typical harasser suggest that there is no typical harasser—despite the popular images such as the lecherous professor, the ladies' man, or even the 'man-eater' (for the woman harasser).

However, while there may not be a typical harasser, there do appear to be typical patterns of harassment.

Sexual harassment scales

A pioneering series of studies that examined individual differences in male behaviour or psychological make-up that lead to a propensity to harass were conducted by psychologist John Pryor (1983). He started from the premise that severe sexual harassment is similar to rape and devised a self-report measure (the LSH) based on a likelihood to rape scale. Pryor created 10 hypothetical scenarios in which a man had the opportunity to harass a woman. Pryor created male characters who, by virtue of their social roles (or the particular circumstances of the scenario), had the power to control a reward or a punishment to the woman concerned. Respondents in his study were asked to place themselves in the role of these men and to consider what they would do in the given situations. Additionally, they were told that they would suffer no negative consequences, regardless of what they did. After analysing each scenario, the respondents had to indicate the likelihood that they would choose among various courses of action, including sexual exploitation of the woman. Examples of the scenario and the likelihood measure are illustrated in Table 5-3.

Table 5-3 *A sample scenario from Pryor's* Likelihood to Sexually Harass *study*

Imagine that you are the news director for a local television station. Due to some personnel changes you have to replace the anchorwoman for the evening news. Your policy has always been to promote reporters from within your organisation when an anchorwoman vacancy occurs. There are several female reporters from which to choose. All are young, attractive and apparently qualified for the job. One reporter, Loretta W., is someone whom you personally find very sexy. You initially hired her, giving her a first break in the TV news business. How likely are you to do the following things in this situation?

Assuming that you fear no reprisals in your job, would you offer Loretta the job in exchange for sexual favours?

Not at all likely   1   2   3   4   5   Very likely

This study was administered to a sample of university men and scored on this measure of 'likelihood to sexually harass'. These scores were related to scores on several other scales, including sex-role stereotyping, adversarial attitudes to women, acceptance of rape myths, and the likelihood to commit rape (based on Malamuth's rape proclivity scale). The study showed that men who scored highly on the LSH scale were also likely to hold rigid sex-role stereotypes, and unlikely to be pro-feminist and lacking in empathy (the ability to take the point of point of view of the other person). The study concluded that the man likely to initiate serious sexual harassment is one who emphasises social and sexual dominance and is not sensitive to others' feelings or perspectives.

Researchers Carl Bartling and Russell Eisenman extended Pryor's work by devising a sexual harassment proclivity scale. The first difference between their scale and Pryor's is that the former can also be administered to women. They argue that men may be the victims of sexual harassment and less likely to report it. The Sexual Harassment Proclivities measure (SHP) consisted of 30 questions which the respondent has to answer by indicating on a scale from 1 (strongly disagree) to 5 (strongly agree). The statements were constructed to reflect the EEOC definitions of sexual harassment. Additional measures such as a sexual activity scale, the Likelihood to Rape scale and scales that assessed sex-role stereotyping were included.

The authors found that of all the scales, the one measuring adversarial sexual beliefs had the strongest relationship to their SHP measure. They also found that the personality profiles for those likely to initiate sexually harassing behaviours appear to be similar for men and women. Adversarial sexual beliefs and weak empathy skills may predispose both men and women to initiate sexual harassment behaviours, including sexual exploitation.

It appears that, at least in the experimental situation, scales to measure tendencies to sexually harass may tease out employees with exploitative proclivities and it is suggested that there may be some possible scope to use such scales as part of an intervention designed to reduce sexual harassment.

Harassers and harassment

So far we have discussed the arguments for and against the existence of a prototypical harasser. What this analysis does not tell us is how many harassers there are, as opposed to how much harassment occurs. By their nature, studies that focus on harassment from a target's point of view (these are the majority of studies) tell us little about how many harassers there are. For example, it is possible that the majority of harassed women are harassed by a small minority of men. This possibility was explored in an interesting study by Louise Fitzgerald and her colleagues (1988) that targeted 235 male academics in a prestigious US university. The academics represented all faculty ranks and also a wide range of ages and academic disciplines. They were asked 22 ingenious questions about sexual harassment that disguised the true purpose of the research study. Pairs of similar questions were put to the academics, the first part asking if that person had been the target of a sexually harassing behaviour, while the second part asked if they had ever behaved in this way to a student. For example, 'Has a student ever made an unsolicited attempt to stroke, caress or touch you?', followed by 'Have you ever attempted to stroke, caress or touch a student?'. These questions were interspersed with other questions on friendship and mentoring.

The results revealed that mentoring and friendship were the most frequent behaviours. This point noted, as many as 37 per cent indicated they had attempted to initiate a personal relationship with a student. Of these, 40 per cent said that this behaviour was directed exclusively at female students. More than 25 per cent of the sample admitted to having dated students and a larger percentage said that they had engaged in sexual relationships with students. Interestingly, only one respondent admitted to ever having sexually harassed a student. A small number reported that some students had initiated sexual relationships or encounters, including 6 per cent who believed they themselves had been sexually harassed. On close examination of these latter cases, it was found that these lecturers were also more likely to have been engaged in sexual relationships with students. Perhaps when they were referring to the women who had harassed them, they were referring to students who had previously dated them, but had now been cast aside. This point is, however, speculative. Overall, the study showed young and older men alike, across all faculties, were just as likely to harass.

Should firms screen out harassers?

This chapter has shown that the typical harasser scarcely differs from the typical worker, except perhaps with regard to certain beliefs and attitudes. Given that most firms already employ selection tools such as personality tests to aid the selection process, the obvious question becomes whether or not it is possible to screen out harassers. The fact that such procedures should not be used as they are not entirely accurate is similar to the equally valid arguments against almost any form of personnel selection (including the use of personality tests). In choosing a selection tool, firms must balance the possibility of excluding potentially valuable employees against the risk of hiring undesirable employees. This is a far-from-exact process and errors are inevitable. If a firm sees the elimination of harassment as an important goal then there may be scope for trying to develop some aspect of the selection process designed to assess the attitudes and beliefs of potential employees. However, such a process is still in its infancy and we would suggest that until there is further progress in developing appropriate tests that this is a temptation that should be resisted, unless of course there are other overriding concerns.

In addition to the personalities of potential harassers there are a host of other factors (such as corporate culture) that can predict whether or not an organisation contains individuals prone to sexual harassment. This issue was addressed in Chapter 4 when describing the person/situation explanation. It may be far easier (and more accurate) to address these other issues before experimenting with an attempt to screen out harassers, since screening is not yet sufficiently advanced to guarantee successful results. We will return to these issues in Chapter 7.

chapter six

The consequences of sexual harassment

The objectives of this chapter are:

to explore how men and women respond to and cope with sexual harassment

to examine the emotional, physiological, social and work-related consequences of sexual harassment

to examine the consequences of sexual harassment to organisations.

How would you respond if you were sexually harassed? For many people the most obvious answer is that they would either confront the harasser or report that person to a higher authority. To do nothing seems inconceivable. Because of such preconceptions, it is not surprising to learn that when Anita Hill made her accusations against Clarence Thomas (see Chapter 1) her credibility came under intense scrutiny. Why had she not reported the incidents when they had occurred? Why had she waited until Thomas was in the public eye (following his possible appointment to the Supreme Court)? In the eyes of much of the public, these concerns led to an inevitable conclusion, namely, that the accusations were false.

In this chapter we examine how people respond to sexual harassment. We begin by considering the strategies that workers have adopted to cope with sexual harassment. It will be shown that the most common reaction to sexual harassment is, in fact, to do nothing. Despite confident assertions that we would undoubtedly take action, there are a variety of factors that may mitigate against such a course of action, including a fear of reprisals, fear of not being believed, as well as uncertainty over whether an action was harassment or just an innocent behaviour that has been misinterpreted. We will then discuss the consequences of sexual harassment for the harassed, the harasser and the organisation. We will show that the effects of harassment can be seen in two interrelated domains: the psychological and the organisational.

Coping with sexual harassment

To date there have been few studies of how workers react to sexual harassment. In part, this is due to problems in identifying those who have experienced harassment, since both formal and informal complaints are relatively rare. Some researchers have tried to overcome this problem by asking people to speculate on how they would react if they were harassed. For example, David Terpstra and Douglas Baker presented male and female students with a list of 18 harassment scenarios and asked how they would react in each case. Their responses were sorted into 'reaction categories'. These included: *leaving the field* (quitting the job or asking for a transfer), *external report* (reporting the incident to local agency or taking legal action), *internal report* (report to supervisor or manager), *physical reaction* (slap, hit or physically resist), *alteration* (change self, behaviour or clothes, or change the environment), *negative verbal confrontation* (ridicule, curse, scream or verbally attack), *positive verbal confrontation* (ask to stop, talk or discuss), *avoidance* (avoid person and area), ignore/do nothing (no action), and other reactions (give in, be flattered).

Analysis of the frequency of such reactions showed that there were three main chosen responses, with verbal confrontation being the most popular choice (24 per cent said would choose this course of action), followed by internal report (20 per cent) and ignore or do nothing (15 per cent). Each of the remaining categories received 7 per cent endorsement or less.

The results of this study are informative, not because they tell us how people actually react to sexual harassment, but rather how they *believe* people should react.

This study amply supports the widespread belief that if a individual is harassed then he or she would complain or take some form of action. Complaining is equated with unwelcomeness (the defining factor of sexual harassment), silence is equated with acquiescence. This pattern of responses suggests that credibility is enhanced if an accusation is made immediately after an incident. As Anita Hill discovered, delayed accusations tend to be viewed sceptically.

Although Terpstra and Baker's response categories are logical, intuitive and apparently exhaustive, they are, of course, hypothetical. What people say they would do and what happens in reality are often quite different. This point was underlined by the results of the USMSPB's studies into sexual harassment. In these studies those who had been harassed were asked how they had reacted to their harassment. Even though the categories were somewhat arbitrary, they shed some interesting light on how people react when they are harassed. Table 6-1 summarises the findings of these studies.

Table 6-1 *How men and women react to sexual harassment*

Reaction to harassment	% of respondents	
	Women	*Men*
(a) USMSPB (1981)		
Ignored behaviour/did nothing	61	65
Avoided the person	48	39
Asked/told person to stop	48	30
Made a joke of the behaviour	31	32
Reported behaviour to supervisor	14	8
Told/threatened to tell other workers	11	6
Went along with the behaviour	6	14
Filed formal grievance	3	2

Reaction to harassment   % of respondents

	Women	Men
(b) USMSPB (1988)		
Ignored behaviour/did nothing	52	42
Avoided the person	43	31
Asked/told the person to stop	44	25
Made a joke of the behaviour	20	20
Told/threatened to tell other workers	14	8
Report to supervisor or official	15	7
Went along with the behaviour	4	7
Transferred, disciplined or gave poor performance rating to the harasser	2	3
Other reactions	10	6

In both studies it is clear that the most common reaction to harassment was in fact to do nothing. In the first study, over 60 per cent of respondents said that they had done nothing when harassed and about half reported doing nothing when questioned in the follow-up study. When action was taken it tended to be informal, perhaps telling the person to stop, avoiding the person or threatening to tell other workers. Only a small number of employees reported the harasser to a supervisor and even fewer filed formal grievances. Most of the federal workers in the study were aware of formal methods (filing a grievance or discrimination complaint), however, formal remedies were seldom chosen.

These studies provide confirmation of the lack of correspondence between what people say they would do and what happens in reality. In a laboratory setting, where there are few consequences for stating that a course of action would be taken, it appears that subjects are not able to envisage the realities of dealing with a harasser.

Although the USMSPB studies show how people reacted to harassment, it concentrates on action oriented problem-solving strategies. It neglects truly psychological reactions (such as self-blame), and focuses on assertive reactions as opposed to passive ones. Deriving their data from their large incidence study, including university women and working women, conducted in 1988, Louise Fitzgerald and her colleagues identified 10 distinct response patterns (see Table 6-2).

Table 6-2 *Responses to sexual harassment*

Internally focused strategies

Detachment

The individual utilises a distancing strategy, which includes such things as minimising the situation, treating it like a joke, telling herself it is not really important, and so on.

Denial

The individual denies that the harassment is occurring; she pretends that nothing is happening or that she doesn't notice; she assumes that it won't continue; she tries to forget about it.

Relabelling

The individual reappraises the situation as less threatening; she offers excuses for the harasser (for example, 'He didn't mean to upset me') or interprets the behaviour as flattering.

Illusory control

The individual attempts to gain a sense of control by taking responsibility for the incident, through attributing the harassment to her own behaviour or attire.

Endurance

The individual essentially does nothing; she 'puts up with' the behaviour; either through fear (of retaliation, of hurting the harasser, of not being believed, of being blamed, or of embarrassment) or because she believes that there are no resources available for help.

Externally focused strategies

Avoidance

The individual attempts to avoid the situation by staying away from the harasser (for example, dropping the class, changing advisors, quitting a job).

Assertion/confrontation

The individual refuses sexual or social offers; verbally confronts the harasser; or otherwise makes clear that the behaviour is unwelcome.

Seeking institutional/organisational relief

The individual reports the incident, consults with an appropriate administrator, files a grievance.

Social support

The individual seeks the support of significant others; seeks validation of her perceptions, or acknowledgment of the reality of the occurrence.

Appeasement

The individual attempts to evade the harassment, but without confrontation or assertion. She offers an excuse, or otherwise attempts to placate the harasser.

Each of the strategies identified above has been observed in studies of responses to sexual harassment. For example, in a study of 150 women who worked in blue collar positions in an auto assembly plant, James Gruber and Lars Bjorn (1986) found that 10 per cent of targets used a relabelling strategy, that is, they reinterpreted the incident, so as not to call it harassment. In her study, Barbara Gutek found that many of the harassed workers she questioned found extenuating circumstances for the harasser (such as, 'he felt lonely'), and in an earlier study, Gutek and Jensen (1982) found many women blamed themselves for the harassment. Like rape, sexual harassment can result in feelings of self-blame and guilt on the part of the targets. Only 24 of 135 targets of harassment reported the incident to someone in authority (about 18 per cent). Thirty per cent of harassed women said reporting the incident would hurt them and another 24 per cent were concerned it would hurt the harasser, which contradicts the myth that many (women) make false complaints to get a man in trouble.

When external coping strategies are employed, it is apparent that formal grievances are rare. The *Working Woman* survey by Sandroff (1988) reported that very few employees take formal action (1.4 out of 1000 employees). Of those who do employ external strategies, the most common response is avoidance, which, across studies, is used by about half of harassed employees. Avoidance would include requesting a transfer, changing courses or quitting a job. Another fairly common strategy is appeasement, or avoiding direct confrontation. Louise Fitzgerald cites humour, excuses and delaying as examples of this strategy. A large number of targets seek social support, usually from friends, co-workers and or family. In the first USMSPB study, 68 per cent of the harassed discussed their problem with a co-worker and more than half discussed their experiences with friends and family.

The single most important finding from these studies is that very few employees make a complaint, either informally or formally, to an internal agent (such as a manager or supervisor), or to an external entity when informal approaches have failed.

How coping strategies are chosen

Given that there are a wide variety of coping strategies that can be adopted, some researchers have questioned whether it is possible to link specific responses to certain types of harassment, or to certain types of people. For example, it might be suggested that strategies such as detachment and denial are most commonly seen in cases of harassment by co-workers, or in less severe forms of harassment (noting that severity of harassment is not objectively defined).

However, despite numerous attempts to find any such links, the research results are largely inconclusive. Predicting how a person will respond based on the type of harassment they experience is far from accurate, since there are numerous other relevant considerations, including the personality of the harassed person, the status of the harasser and the organisational context.

Nevertheless, some interesting observations have been made. Gruber and Bjorn (1986) found that the victim's self-esteem influenced their response: people with low self-esteem will usually act more passively. Other personality variables that may have a bearing include holding feminist beliefs or values (making people react more assertively), and Gutek and Jensen (1982) found that those holding traditional sex-role attitudes were more likely to react passively.

Causes and consequences for workers and organisations

To illustrate how men might react to sexual harassment we present two cases in Box 6-1 below. The cases show how difficult it may be for a man to react to a problem which is 'not supposed to happen to them'.

Box 6-1 *Men's reactions to sexual harassment by women*

Case 1

When I was a first year student at university I took a week-end job at a small warehouse stacking and transporting plumbing supplies. Surprisingly I was the only male around (at least at weekends). There was a small office attached to the main warehouse staffed by four women who did clerical work. The youngest was probably in her late twenties, the oldest, probably about 48–50, ordinary looking women, not stunning not ugly either. It started with the younger one, she flirted with me like mad and constantly asked whether she could feel my muscles (I am fairly big and muscular). I thought it was genuine interest, and although I did not fancy her, or wished to pursue a relationship, I was flattered. That is, until one day she turns up with her husband! He took me to one side and told me he knew I chatted her up, and could I please stop doing it!! As weeks went by, this woman, now joined by the others, started making derogatory comments about men in my presence whenever I went into their office. Things like 'men are useless' and 'big men always have tiny pricks'. They also started calling me names like 'lover boy' or 'college boy', for example a common comment would be 'Come over lover boy, show us you are the exception to the rule'. I have been brought up to respect women so I politely told them that their comments were offensive and inappropriate. They just sneered or laughed.

When I finally told the warehouse supervisor he just laughed it off and said 'Come on, son, are you really scared of that lot? These women are sexually deprived. Don't be a wimp, just show them a thing or two'. That summed up his disgusting attitude, as disgusting as those uneducated, crass women. What was I supposed to do? File a formal complaint? I would have been a laughing stock. After 3 months there, I quit.

A 20-year-old, male electronics student

Case 2

I get tired hearing about men harassing women, as in my place of employment I have been subjected to several forms of sexual (and other) harassment by women. In the district office of the Education Department where I work, a third of the staff are male and the rest female.

The harassment is very underhand and part of this empowerment process which the women go on about.

Examples of the harassment include:

1. Not passing on documentation which is meant for general office distribution. This has resulted in me being unable to attend meetings, etc. When asked, it's always 'Oh, I thought I'd given it to you'. When discussed with senior management, they are reluctant to do anything. This reaction is very sad.

2. The other major sexual harassment behaviour consists of discussions in the staff room. The women focus on monthly cycles, and how 'men just don't know what to do with a penis'. This form of conversation is offensive to the male members of staff. One woman is always talking about 'cutting off penises'.

What saddens me is that these women form part of the social justice/gender equality network of which I am also a member. However, they never invite me to participate or contribute to their discussions. It is obvious to me that these women may have had negative experiences with men in the past, but that does not justify their using this as the yardstick by which to measure all men.

A 37-year-old, male education officer

The cases in Box 6-1 are interesting in that the harassment experienced by men is very similar in form to that often experienced by women. Although some argue that the consequences to men are less severe than to women, there are occasions when this is not the case. This point has already been addressed earlier in the book (for example concerning its implications for the definition of sexual harassment) but is worth further consideration here. There may well be occasions when men do find sexual harassment less distressing than women because they have been socialised to interpret advances from women as flattering (similar arguments can be employed when considering the reactions to sexual harassment by women from different cultures). Further, men have also been socialised not to complain, particularly about ill-treatment by women. For example, topics such as battered husbands tend to be ridiculed. One can speculate that matters may be different if sexual harassment was defined by intention rather than effect. One complication in understanding men's reactions to sexual advances is that research studies have shown that men tend to infer sexual motives from behaviours that were intended as non-sexual acts of friendship (see Chapter 4). For example, a woman taking an interest in a male colleague will be treated as exhibiting romantic interest. Given such findings, some writers are quick to dismiss men's claims of sexual harassment as misinterpretations of innocent behaviours. One might further argue that because women are less likely to make such inferences their claims of sexual harassment need to be taken more seriously.

Why workers don't report harassment

So far we have established that most workers do not take formal action against harassers. For example, Gutek found that women often think it takes too much time and effort to make a formal complaint. In her study only 18 per cent reported the harassment to someone with authority. This occurs for a variety of reasons, such as believing that nothing can or will be done. Furthermore, some are reluctant because they do not want to cause problems for the harasser. Additional reasons for not bringing a complaint include fear of retaliation, fear of being humiliated, as well as general fears about harming one's career by being labelled as a troublemaker (see Box 6-2).

Most workers tend to prefer to adopt informal methods of coping which give them a greater feeling of control over the situation, perhaps because they entail less risk. Also, given that sexual harassment behaviour is often ambiguous, some may prefer to err on the side of caution and avoid making a formal complaint. Reporting a person can often result in considerable problems for the accuser, reflected in the USMSPB research that showed that, of those who filed a formal grievance, nearly a third discovered that it simply served to make matters worse (see Box 6-2 for an example) and only 44 per cent of the agencies in question punished the harasser.

Box 6-2 *Staff turnover following sexual harassment*

Case 3

I complained to a female member of staff about the harassment. She told me she had been informed that I was an inefficient and disruptive worker. When I filed a formal complaint about this man, I was told he had not meant any harm and that he had been trying to help me in my new job. My confidence was totally undermined. I knew he had sexually harassed me! I tried everything: being nice, polite, explaining how he made me feel, and finally telling him to f off. Nothing worked. I finally left. I have heard that since I left, 3 years ago, 5 women have also left, 3 having made complaints about him.

A 26-year-old, female therapist in a hospital.

Case 4

I had not mentioned anything to my manager about the harassment incidents, mainly because I thought I had the situation under control but also because I didn't want to cause any trouble for this guy. Ironically, I got fired a few weeks later and branded a troublemaker as I was told 'I gave the men in the shop big erections'.

A 19-year-old, female shop assistant

Bringing a complaint of harassment is certainly fraught with difficulties. Accusers may be branded as troublemakers and the harassers then labelled as the victims. Given such adverse reactions, it becomes easier to understand why workers may be reluctant to make their accusations official. Both employers and the courts should be aware of the fact that direct action against a harasser is not brought easily and that in most cases workers appear reluctant to take action until all other avenues have been exhausted, including behaviours such as ignoring the harasser (see Box 6-3).

Consequences of sexual harassment

Sexual harassment has been found to have a number of effects on the workers who experience it. These consequences can be broadly grouped into four main areas.

Box 6-3 *Ignoring the harassment can lead to problems*

Case 5

At first I laughed off his attention. I hoped that by treating the whole thing lightly he would take the hint that I was not interested. I could not have been more wrong. Evidently my good natured attitude made me more appealing because as time passed the frequency of comments increased and also became more explicitly sexual.

A 21-year-old, female sales assistant

Psychological and emotional

Sexual harassment appears to have strong effects on the psychological status of workers. For example, a study by the Working Women United Institute (WWUI) (1978) found that 78 per cent of harassed women reported having suffered serious emotional consequences. Peggy Crull (1982) looked at the consequences of sexual harassment on 262 women who had sought help from the WWUI. A staggering 90 per cent of them reported suffering psychological stress symptoms—in particular, general tension and nervousness, in addition to feeling anger and fear. Representative studies include one by Loy and Stewart, who surveyed some 500 people in 1984. Three-quarters of those who were harassed reported experiencing distress including nervousness, irritability and uncontrolled anger.

The first USMSPB study found that for about one-third of the women and one-fifth of the men who had been harassed, their emotional and physical condition worsened. Of women who had suffered from actual or attempted rape or assault, the great majority reported a negative toll emotionally and physically. Fear reactions also include lowered self-esteem and self-confidence and a feeling of loss of control. Recently Gutek and Koss (1993) reviewed the research on consequences and found that emotional reactions usually include anger, fear, depression, a feeling of helplessness and vulnerability.

Physiological and medical

The above studies also found evidence of medical or health-related consequences. The Crull study found that women experienced nausea, headaches and tiredness, irritability and crying spells. Loy and Stewart (1984), and Gutek found evidence of negative health consequences including insomnia and weight loss. Recent analysis by Gutek and Koss (1993) found that harassed workers can also experience gastro-intestinal problems, jaw tightness and teeth grinding, binge-eating and headaches.

Social and interpersonal

It is common for the effects of harassment to spill over to other relationships. Gutek found that 15 per cent of the women harassed reported that their relations with colleagues (other men) were affected. Some women displayed their emotions against family members, in particular other males such as husbands or fathers, as seen in greater numbers of divorces and marital problems. Social problems are also manifest at work. In Gutek's study, relationships with other colleagues were affected adversely for nearly a third of the victims. Generally, workers often report problems with other workers following harassment, even though these other workers were not involved in the harassment.

Work related

All of the above factors can, unsurprisingly, have a detrimental influence on job performance. Studies by Crull, the USMSPB and Terpstra and Cook (1985), have all found that those who are harassed experience higher levels of transfers and de-motions than those not harassed. These consequences are easily visible, but there are other related consequences, such as being passed over for promotion and receiving poorer references.

The first USMSPB study found that about 35 per cent of the women harassed reported worsened feelings about their jobs, a figure similar to that found by Gutek in her study. Other feelings include lowered overall job satisfaction, dreading work, less organisational commitment, decreased ability to concentrate and lowered confidence in one's skills and competence.

In addition to the problems faced by those who experience sexual harassment, effects may be seen in other workers. For example, one should not overlook the harassers, who although unlikely to face disciplinary action, may be more likely to be transferred. Further, other workers present in an environment in which harassment is occurring may also show lowered levels of job satisfaction and poorer performance. One interesting aspect of harassment is that colleagues may distance themselves from those experiencing harassment, perhaps out of fear of the harasser or simply not wishing to draw any such harassment onto themselves. Or perhaps, as one case below illustrates, because they believe those who complain are trouble-makers and that their problems are not real. Examples of the consequences of sexual harassment are given in Box 6-4 below.

Box 6-4 *Consequences of sexual harassment*

Case 6

What disgusted me the most were other women, all married with children. They thought that even after the incident I should be flattered that he paid so much attention to me.

A 27-year-old, female catering assistant at a hospital

Case 7

I had been working for him for 2–3 months when it all started, at first it was just the way he looked at me, but then he would compliment my clothes and my hair but I didn't think much about it I thought he was just being pleasant but then one day I was stood on a chair in his office putting away a file and suddenly I felt his hands on my hips helping me down and then he tried to kiss me so I pushed him away telling him that I was a married woman and I wasn't interested and we just left it at that, no more was said about it and I just put it down to a middle aged man having a mid life crisis and for a few months everything was fine he was his normal charming self and then one day he made another pass at me this time someone else came into the office to witness this so then the whole office thought we were having an affair. I was so scared that someone would tell my husband who I loved very much so I ended up leaving a job that meant a lot to me. I realised maybe it was partly my fault, if I had dressed down and hadn't been so friendly, this might not have happened.

A 34-year-old, female accountant

Case 8

I deal on the phone with this male insurance broker. When the receptionist puts him through to me the first thing he says is 'Hello, pornographic Paula'. He usually goes on to say how he dreamt about me the night before. One day I had to phone him to report a particular financial case from which he did rather well. 'Oh, Paula, that is great news, if you were here, I'd come all over you'. That sort of comment is degrading, humiliating and absolutely filthy. I feel like slamming the phone down on him, but how can I? I am supposed to respect this guy for bringing us in business. If I ever put the phone down, my boss would come down on me like a tonne of bricks. There is really no way out.

A 27-year-old, female insurance consultant in an insurance firm

Case 9

When he made those comments I just stared into space. After two months of his harassment I noticed a change in my relationship with my husband. I became moody, terse, I did not want sex anymore. I was in tears most evenings. In my country if this happens to a woman, you just accept it, but here my husband says, you are supposed to complain as it is a big offence. Eventually I did complain and two weeks later I was fired after being told my work was not up to good standards.

A 41-year-old, female graphic designer

Case 10

My first boss, a woman, harassed me. Even though it sounds crazy, I now believe it was sexual harassment, because even though she was not a lesbian or ever propositioned me, she used to run me down with sexual slurs. She used to call me a 'slag', 'frigid', 'androgynous looking', etc. She constantly told me off because of the way I dressed, and said that she could tell when I had a period because I 'smelt like a bleeding cow'. After a while I told her how I felt as politely as I could, but she hardly took any notice. I was a young, country girl and I was impressed by her status and impeccable dress. She made me feel really small. I don't know what her motives were, but with hindsight I believe she realised I was or could become better at the job than her.

A 40-year-old, female biochemist

Case 11

This marketing manager harassed these two secretaries and this homosexual boy (he was a trainee on placement). He called the girls stupid names like 'darling flower' 'sweetpea' and so forth and gave them hints about how to sexually satisfy their boyfriends. The girls just giggled in his presence and cursed him when he was not around. He also teased the trainee about his sexuality and told him to f these girls because that would 'cure him'. For me and my colleagues it made a strained, unpleasant atmosphere. I guess we were too chicken to confront this guy. One day the trainee decided enough was enough and beat the manager up outside the office (after work). Surprisingly, the manager took no reprisals, at least not immediately. The atmosphere improved a little for a while. When the trainee left, we heard he had received a poor evaluation. I had worked with him and believed he was very good.

A 35-year-old, male marketing consultant in a manufacturing firm

Consequences to the organisation

There is little doubt that sexual harassment is an extremely costly problem for organisations. According to the USMSPB reports, sexual harassment cost the Federal US Government an estimated US$267 million during the period between May 1985 and May 1987. This figure represents the costs of replacing employees who left their jobs ($36.7 million), paying sick leave to employees who missed work ($26.1 million), and reduced individual and group productivity ($204.5 million). In the private sector, the *Working Woman* survey (1988) found that a typical *Fortune 500* company (with 23 000 employees) loses in the region of US$6.7 million per annum. It is also likely to be the case that there are other, less obvious, financial consequences for organisations, as illustrated in Box 6-5.

Box 6-5 *Organisations may lose business*

Case 12

My partner and I commission firms to make prints and other art works. It is not unusual for a small firm to do rather well from our commissioning. One day one of these firms invited me to see their new printing offices. The bosses (two men) were very polite and chatty. We had a light lunch in one office and later I asked where the toilet was. I walked down a long corridor, and ended up in this printing and photocopying room they had not shown me. There I really got my shock. The walls were covered with an assortment of pin-ups—naked girls in explicit poses. I really did not expect this, dealing with professional people. My respect for them vanished in seconds. Yes, this company produced good work, and had I been a male I may have 'forgiven them'. But I figured there were other good companies out there. So this firm lost us as clients and thousands of dollars for good.

A 48-year-old, female business owner

These figures are of obvious concern to any organisation. Sexual harassment is a financial drain, not simply because of litigation costs, but most significantly because it reduces the ability of workers to do their jobs, decreasing levels of interest and commitment, leading to lowered productivity and higher levels of absenteeism. Problems such as dismissing workers, transfers and resignations will also hinder organisational efficiency. Other problems may be manifest in denied promotions and decreased training opportunities. Nevertheless, it is litigation (and the ensuing legal costs, together with bad publicity) that probably arouse the strongest concerns in organisations. We will discuss in the following chapter a proactive strategy aimed at the prevention of sexual harassment (largely through training) that is far less costly than the reactive strategy of waiting for cases to occur and then taking action against any transgressors. The costs of sexual harassment are often hidden in statistics such as staff turnover. Unless one actively looks for evidence of sexual harassment, it is unlikely that its occurrence will become apparent. As discussed, most people who are harassed take no formal action, and may well leave their jobs rather than making an accusation.

As a final comment, it is worth considering that sexual harassment will rarely thrive in an environment where attempts are made to safeguard workers, and conversely, it will flourish in an environment that appears to tolerate, or even encourage such behaviour. The recent case of the Mitsubishi car manufacturing plant in Chicago (see Box 6-6) highlights how sexual harassment can reach epidemic proportions if the 'right' conditions are present.

Box 6-6 *The worst ever case of sexual harassment?*

Car men's 'green light to grope'

Bosses at a Japanese-owned car firm have been accused of letting male employees sexually harass 700 female staff. A US government lawsuit which could cost the company millions of dollars alleges women at the Mitsubishi factory near Chicago were systematically fondled and submitted to humiliating comments by colleagues from assembly line workers to middle managers. The Equal Employment Opportunity Commission says executives knew what was going on and tolerated it in the world's worst sex harassment case. A separate private suit filed by 30 women says the Japanese management routinely took male employees to live sex shows during overseas training sessions and complained that women did not belong in factories. It alleges that male workers and supervisors kissed and fondled women, displayed sexual graffiti, demanded sexual acts and retaliated against those who refused. 'This is the worst, most pervasive case you'll see', said Patricia Benassi, one of the women's lawyers. 'Men who stepped forward and tried to help women were themselves retaliated against.' Paul Igasaki, Equal Employment Opportunity Commission vice-chairman said the case was being taken to court because efforts to negotiate and end to the harassment had failed. Each female employee could collect £200,000 damages if the commission proves its case. Those in the private suit could get more. Mitsubishi vice president Gary Schultz said: 'Discrimination of any kind will never, and has never, been tolerated in this plant. We find harassment in the workplace to be reprehensible'.

Source: Article by George Gordon in *The Daily Mail*, 10 April 1996.

part three

Prevention and future directions

chapter seven

Management attitudes and the prevention of sexual harassment

The objectives of this chapter are:

to examine management attitudes to sexual harassment

to discuss the strategies that government and organisations can use to prevent and deal with sexual harassment

to suggest a plan of action to prevent sexual harassment.

In Chapter 4 it was argued that the organisational culture can influence the extent to which sexual harassment will be present in the workplace. Consequently, changing the organisational culture is one way that management can take steps towards the eradication of sexual harassment. It is not a problem that cannot be solved, nor is it inevitable in certain workplaces. In this chapter we discuss some of the ways in which managers can try to reduce sexual harassment in the workplace. We begin by considering one of the most important, yet easily overlooked, factors that will influence the extent of sexual harassment—management attitudes. This is important because the attitudes of managers will influence the behaviour of their employees. Even the most carefully thought out campaign to eradicate sexual harassment will be undermined if managers convey an impression that they consider the problem to be trivial, or irrelevant to their workplace. We then consider some of the practical steps that organisations can take as part of a policy to reduce sexual harassment. This will include the need to carry out research amongst employees to establish the extent to which a problem exists, the creation of training schemes and finally evaluations of training. We also consider the inadequate nature of existing legislation and the need for clearer definitions of sexual harassment.

'It doesn't happen here'

Although public and organisational awareness of sexual harassment has increased over the years, organisations have often been slow to adopt effective guidelines. For example, in 1980 the EEOC in the US published the first guidelines on sexual harassment. However, management expert Jeanette Cleveland reported that by the following year only 29 per cent of organisations surveyed had policies regarding sexual harassment. By 1987, this figure had risen to 97 per cent. In most cases these policies suggested a course of action to be taken by the person being harassed, such as reporting it to their supervisor.

The aptly titled *Harvard Business Review* (*HBR*) survey, 'Sexual harassment: Some see it…some won't', was particularly interesting as an indication of management attitudes in the early 1980s (Collins and Blodgett 1981). There were some 2 000 subscribers who responded to the survey. The results showed that many respondents, including senior managers, were often out of touch with the scale of harassment. Many managers believed that the problem had been magnified out of all proportion and that it did not occur as frequently as some people (notably women) alleged. Managers were quoted as saying:

> This entire subject is a perfect example of a minor special interest group's ability to blow up any 'issue' to a level of importance which in no way relates to the reality of the world in which we live and work.
>
> *38-year-old, male plant manager for a large manufacturer of industrial goods, p. 77.*

I am baffled by this issue. I used to believe it was a subject that was being exaggerated by paranoid women and sensational journalists. Now I think the problem is real but somewhat overdrawn. My impression is that my own company is relatively free of sexual harassment. But I don't know the facts.

A 53-year-old, male, senior vice president of a medium-sized financial institution, p. 78.

The main findings of this study with respect to management attitudes were that many managers in the US thought that the severity and frequency of sexual harassment were overrated (two-thirds of the men and about half of the women). The generally pessimistic attitudes were reflected in the limited steps taken to deal with sexual harassment. Table 7-1 below is taken from a summary of the *HBR* results compiled by Collins and Blodgett.

Table 7-1 *Management attitudes and policies on sexual behaviour in the workplace*

Policy	Do you favour this policy?	Does your company have this policy?
	%	%
A management statement to all employees disapproving of sexual harassment	73	29
A management statement disapproving of office flirtations, even when mutual	28	9
Developing appropriate sanctions for sexual harassers	68	**17**
Orientation programs to make all new employees aware of company policy on sexual behaviour at work	59	**13**

Policy	Do you favour this policy?	Does your company have this policy?
	%	%
Developing materials—employee manuals, films, and so forth—to make all employees aware of this issue	44	8
A management directive that asks each department head to take responsibility for preventing sexual harassment in his or her department	68	16

Source: from Collins and Blodgett (1981).

Other studies conducted during the course of the 1980s confirmed this generally poor situation. For example, US authors Constance Backhouse and Leah Cohen (1982) encountered hostility, lack of co-operation and at best a dismissive attitude towards sexual harassment on the part of management of several organisations. Similarly, Barbara Gutek's survey results also revealed a dismissive attitude towards sexual harassment as a major issue. Gutek found that less than 5 per cent of respondents thought it was a major problem.

Although public attitudes seem to have improved with time, organisations still cling to the belief that sexual harassment is a marginal non-issue. In 1990, 1000 top British firms were surveyed by management experts Marilyn Davidson and Jill Earnshaw (1990) (see Table 7-2).

The study also found that 88 per cent of personnel directors had not issued a policy statement regarding management's attitude to sexual harassment and only 21 per cent said training was given to those responsible for implementing the policy. These findings suggest that attitudes towards sexual harassment have altered (for the better) since 1980, but there is clearly still room for further improvement. Even when organisations do appear to be taking the problem seriously, it is often the case that they are merely paying lip service to the existing legislation. In our research for

Sexual Harassment we encountered a large number of firms who would not discuss their policies and procedures for dealing with sexual harassment. In some cases this was because no such policies existed, but in other cases it was probably because the organisations would rather not look too closely at the preventative steps they have taken, for fear that they might realise their weaknesses.

Table 7-2 *Attitudes of personnel directors towards sexual harassment*

Preventative measures and support systems	% of personnel directors in favour
Publicity given to legal and other remedies currently available to victims	86
Measures to promote awareness of the problem	80.2
Support given to women's organisations and others providing skilled assistance to victims	74.3
More empirical research further documenting the extent of sexual harassment at work	63.6
Stronger legislation prohibiting sexual harassment at work with appropriate legal sanctions	30.2

Source: from Davidson and Earnshaw (1990).

As mentioned in Chapter 3, we encountered a number of companies who have tried to address issues such as prevalence by asking their employees solitary questions such as 'Have you ever been sexually harassed?'. Although this is in some ways commendable, it hardly forms a sound basis for the conclusion that an organisation is free from sexual harassment, since the question is highly ambiguous and victims rarely draw attention to themselves. Unfortunately, it appears that some firms are well aware of the limitations to such an approach, but having included such an item in a survey, feel that they have gone some way to fulfilling the obligations imposed on them by government legislation. In other words, they have done the bare minimum required to establish a concern for the problem, yet not enough to actually uncover the existence of any problem. In other cases, it seemed sufficient to have created a pamphlet or poster, which was also taken as having fulfilled the requirements of legislation. In such instances, the companies concerned are sticking to the letter of the law, if not the spirit. Until such time as the legislation is improved, this situation looks set to continue.

In summary, it appears that management attitudes towards sexual harassment have improved over the last 20 years and that real progress has been made in recognising the existence of a serious problem. It is still, however, an issue that can be easily dismissed by sceptical managers. As stated earlier, management attitudes are important determinants of organisational culture, which in turn influences levels of harassment. By denying the existence of the problem and denigrating it as a trivial issue, managers may inadvertently be introducing the conditions in which such behaviour can flourish.

Dealing with sexual harassment

There are two main levels at which we can attempt to deal with sexual harassment. First, through government legislation, and second, through organisational interventions.

Legislation

In many countries (such as Australia, the US and the UK) sexual harassment is categorised as an offence under sexual discrimination acts. This has occurred for historical as well as pragmatic reasons. In the last few years, legislation has significantly improved for the better. For example, in Australia the requirement that harassment has tangible consequences for the person being harassed has been removed. Further, the notion of vicarious liability has been introduced, whereby employers are made responsible for delivering guidelines to employees. In effect, organisations are now obliged to act against sexual harassment. These changes have served to make it easier to report acts of sexual harassment and for individuals to take legal action against both harassers and organisations which have not safeguarded their employees.

Although legislation has improved, there is still some way to go in refining existing legislation. Including sexual harassment under sexual discrimination law can result in some clear cases of harassment going unpunished, when offenders can claim that they have harassed both males and females. In such cases, the offensive behaviour cannot logically be said to be sexual discrimination, since the offender has 'discriminated' against both sexes. This sounds ludicrous, but there has been at least one case in which this has resulted in the acquittal of an alleged harasser (see Chapter 4). Sexual harassment clearly needs specific legislation, which recognises that it can take many different forms and occur for many different reasons. We return to this issue in the following chapter.

Another issue that needs to be addressed is how to interpret an organisation's claim to have taken reasonable steps to prevent sexual harassment. In Australia, for example, there are no enforceable guidelines on what steps an organisation must take to comply with the existing legislation. It may be sufficient to distribute a small pamphlet on the subject and nothing else. Either through ignorance or indifference, firms can easily comply with the minimum requirements of the legislation.

Generally, governments have some way to go in clarifying what constitutes sexual harassment and in suggesting ways for organisations to take effective action against it. In Australia, the existing legislation contains a number of ambiguities—most obviously that of the 'reasonable person' standard. This is an ambiguous term that can be interpreted in numerous ways. When an officer at the HREOC in Sydney was asked to explain the 'reasonable person' standard, the officer was unable to explain it clearly, suggesting it was 'something to do with vicarious liability'. After some prompting, we were assured that it was different from the 'reasonable person' standard in the US, although a reading of the legislation suggested the contrary. If members of the HREOC are unable to explain the terms of sexual harassment legislation clearly, then it is hardly surprising that organisations cannot make sense of it.

Recently (October 1996), the HREOC has introduced new codes which attempt to clarify the existing legislation. The new codes try to provide firms with guidelines as to the 'bottom line' of their responsibilities. For example, it empha-sises that employers must set up internal processes to prevent harassment; that a clear written policy must be made available to all staff; that there should be education campaigns and staff appointed to give advice; and that generally, 'all reasonable steps' must be taken to prevent sexual harassment.

Organisational interventions

To date, there has not been any systematic effort to evaluate the effectiveness of the widely differing forms of interventions that organisations can adopt. There is a great deal of advice on what steps might be taken, but there is no evidence (not even anecdotal) to suggest how resources might be allocated most efficiently. Nevertheless, one might reasonably expect that some of these interventions might either reduce levels of harassment, or make it easier to take action against offenders.

The first step an organisation can take is to *recognise that harassment is a pervasive and costly issue*. Denying its existence ensures that it will thrive, albeit undetected by senior management. It is particularly important to recognise the *harassment* and not just the *sexual* aspects of the problem.

The organisation should then *propose a definition of sexual harassment*. As discussed in Chapter 2, this is a far from straightforward problem and may be coloured by the particular concerns of an organisation. Typically, definitions have included highly ambiguous terms (such as *unwanted*) which can be interpreted in widely different ways. The alternative approach of listing unacceptable behaviours may seem a more concrete step, but this too can be fraught with similar ambiguities. Even though an accurate definition may be elusive, it is important that organisations convey to their employees that sexual harassment (however it is defined) will not be tolerated in the workplace.

Organisations may take advantage of an obvious resource in developing guidelines, namely their employees. As discussed earlier, senior managers and personnel officers do not always have accurate perceptions of the problems within their organisation and may take actions that inadvertently accentuate problems rather than remedying them. For example, one problem the authors encountered was that managers would appoint individuals as 'sexual harassment officers' (the person complainants should contact), not realising that they had appointed a person who was responsible for harassing their colleagues. This leaves management believing that they have taken a firm stance against harassment, and employees helpless to take any action. Cases in which this happens are common. This highlights a simple problem whereby interventions serve to instil a false sense of security within organisations and may exacerbate the problem rather than curing it.

Once a policy against harassment has been put forward, organisations must then *consider the process by which grievances should be reported and acted upon.* Some companies (such as the Corning Corporation in the US) have proposed that those being harassed should informally inform the harasser that their behaviour is unacceptable, before proceeding with a formal complaint. The role of the employer becomes pivotal only after the parties have exhausted private opportunities to resolve the matter.

This may be helpful in some cases of sexual harassment, but given the harassed's given tendency to remain silent, will probably only encourage them to continue to remain so. Confronting a harasser is unlikely to be an easy decision and most workers would rather say nothing (see Chapter 6).

The other alternative, where harassment is reported to a neutral third party (either within the organisation or outside), is a better strategy. Recently, the University of Queensland introduced a scheme whereby independent sexual harassment conciliators were introduced to investigate complaints. However, with such procedures care must be taken to ensure that alleged harassers *can* be contacted informally before any formal action is taken, otherwise accusations of witch-hunts are possible. The most significant example of a third party investigation was that carried out by Commissioner Carmel Niland in her investigation of the allegations against Terry Griffiths. Without such a confidential third party, it is highly unlikely that the witnesses would have been forthcoming with their allegations.

The single most important aspect in the complaints process is that *those reporting harassment are treated sympathetically*. In the vast majority of cases, workers reporting sexual harassment will describe a systematic pattern of harassment, not an isolated incident which could have been an innocent action. Most people who are harassed will initially give offenders the benefit of the doubt. It is only when actions are repeated, or perhaps put together with other forms of harassment, that a person being harassed will define their experience as harassment.

In any cases of alleged harassment, the grievance procedures should reflect a concern for both the person being harassed as well as the alleged harasser. In Australia, there have been cases in which innocent workers have been placed on suspension for several months pending the outcome of investigations. Western legal systems are based on the premise that it is better that a hundred guilty people go free, rather than one innocent person be convicted. Organisations are largely free to turn this premise on its head should they wish to do so, but the effects on organisational culture and worker morale are likely to be highly detrimental. Solving one problem could simply lead to a host of other equally serious problems.

Other interventions against sexual harassment are possible, but may be too complicated (or controversial) to implement. For example, personnel selection might attempt to screen out candidates with sexist or discriminatory views, or might check references for past allegations of harassment. Unfortunately, until we can more accurately predict which people are likely to harass (if indeed this is ever a realistic possibility) or rely on references to accurately reveal a person's past misconduct, then such procedures appear unlikely to be successfully introduced.

Training and materials

We now consider the steps an organisation can take when implementing a policy against sexual harassment. This represents an idealised scenario that needs to be modified by the requirements of the specific organisations concerned, as well as by time and financial constraints.

Step 1: Needs assessment

Does sexual harassment occur in the organisation? Training starts with a needs assessment. Sexual harassment would not necessarily be the only issue to be tackled at this time. Related issues, such as general discrimination, ill-treatment and bullying might also be included. Employers could distribute questionnaires concerning sexual harassment (for example, Fitzgerald's Sexual Experiences Questionnaire or the SHWI in Appendix I, and organisational culture (possibly using the Tolerance for Sexual Harassment Inventory). Once again, we stress that isolated questions such as 'Have you been sexually harassed?' produce *meaningless results* and encourage complacency. The questionnaires can be administered by the organisation itself, although an external body might offer the advantages of knowledge of questionnaire design and impartiality.

Step 2: Collating results

The survey may reveal that the organisation has a single distinct pattern of harassment—for example, displays such as pin-ups. If there do not appear to be major problems, a general training program with existing materials may be adequate.

Step 3: Deliver training

Training can take many forms, but generally should involve a degree of interaction. Simply showing a video on sexual harassment without discussing the issues it raises is unlikely to influence behaviour. Workers should be encouraged to discuss the topic with either colleagues or with independent trainers. For a fuller discussion of the exact content of such interventions we refer the reader to the manual by Suzy Nixon and Julie Roberts, *Dealing with Sexual Harassment* (1992). This describes ways in which trainers can interact with staff, as well as details of how conciliation can be structured. Workers may provide feedback on the usefulness of these sessions, but this should not be confused with the final stage of the process, evaluation.

Step 4: Evaluation and changes

Training must be evaluated. Hiring consultants and giving employees time off from regular duties are both expensive and time-consuming. Organisations should expect to see some measurable effects of training and this can only be established some weeks or months after the delivery of training. The organisation might consider redistributing the incidence questionnaire (see Step 1) at regular intervals to monitor improvements. It may be necessary to modify training in the light of these results. For example, organisations may need to develop stricter sanctions for offenders.

One final issue concerning training relates to the problems faced by large organisations where training the entire workforce is a virtual impossibility. In such cases, it has come to our attention that organisations may use training in lieu of sanctions. That is, individuals who have been identified as harassers (through complaints) are sent on training courses without ever being told that their past conduct has caused concern. Such individuals are unlikely to be receptive to training and may even disrupt the training of others. Such practices come about because organisations are unsure of how to proceed following an initial accusation and hope that the training initiative will prevent further complaints. If there are further complaints then severe disciplinary action, such as dismissal, may be made easier by virtue of having provided this form of 'warning'.

As an illustration of how firms can adopt relatively clear policies for dealing with sexual harassment, we have included a copy of the guidelines issued by the UK Employment Department (see Appendix II). These guidelines are generally exhaustive and consider issues that are often ignored, such as being aware of the feelings that the harassed may experience and the fact that sexual harassment may be a problem even if it is not obvious.

Conclusion

While there are a number of steps an organisation can take towards dealing with sexual harassment, there is little information to suggest how effective such interventions might be. Organisations wishing to take action must therefore resort to guesswork and instinct in tackling the problem. This can result in a myriad of approaches that are impossible to compare with one another. For example, sexual harassment has been defined and measured in a variety of ways that make it impossible to integrate findings. Similarly, organisational policies vary considerably.

One common example of just how widely organisational policies can differ concerns the treatment of 'romantic' relationships within the workplace. Some organisations have developed sexual harassment policies that forbid relationships between employees. Within some organisations males may be advised to only meet with female colleagues when others are present, or to leave the door open. Often unnecessarily extreme and largely unjustified measures are devised, particularly when the prevention of sexual harassment is given as the justification. Those responsible for such policies have placed the *sexual* before the *harassment* and probably do not fully understand the nature of this problem.

At this time organisations are often reluctant to directly address sexual harassment because they fear embarrassment and bad publicity. There is a tendency to conceal cases, sometimes to the extent of punishing the victims, rather than the offenders. Much of the blame for this unfortunate situation rests with poor legislation and guidelines. While it may take years for governments to revise legislation, the Australian model encourages organisations to take proactive measures to deal with the problem. Nevertheless, this 'encouragement' lacks any real power and even organisations committed to safeguarding their workers may be lulled into a false sense of security by believing that simple steps such as publishing a policy statement have an impact on workplace behaviours.

chapter eight

The future of sexual harassment

It is 20 years since the term 'sexual harassment' was first employed. In that time, the term has been interpreted in a number of different ways. One of the recurring themes in this book is that the divergent interpretations given to the topic have served to undermine the seriousness with which individuals and organisations address it. In our final chapter we argue that what is currently required is that the term 'sexual harassment' be broken down into a series of more meaningful components that will allow effective legislation to be developed. Until this is done, the ambiguity of legislation in most countries ensures that the topic will continue as a source of confusion and possibly bad feeling in workplaces, as organisations struggle to interpret legal requirements.

One man's interpretation of sexual harassment

Confront a politically correct woman and she'll say that men 'just don't get it'. She'll be wrong of course. Men understand that sexual harassment is simply a bogus invention used to fuel bad political rhetoric. Reasonable men recognise that genuine sexual harassment actually involves two wildly different transgressions, namely extortion and bad manners.

It's extortion when a man says to a female colleague or subordinate, 'give me a blow job and make it a hummer or tomorrow you'll be out of here.'

It's bad manners when a man says to a subordinate, 'nice hooters, hon', or whines for a date or plays Siskel and Ebert with *Longdongophobia*...

Here's the news: Women really do seek to gain the attention of men. Shocking yet true. Some women—maybe nobody you know personally— actually hope the right guy will initiate a conversation that will lead, ultimately, to a badly wanted sexual advance. Sexual provocation and sexual harassment are sometimes officemates…

Men, perforce, are empiricists when it comes to experiments in sexual chemistry: It's all trial and error, with errors outnumbering successes 20 to one. Men just hope that when rejection comes, it won't be extraordinarily painful. Certainly, they hope it won't come with an arrest warrant (Boyles 1991).

These views of Denis Boyles on sexual harassment were published in an issue of *Playboy* magazine. The sentiments expressed are likely to sadden anyone with any real knowledge or understanding of this issue. They represent a badly slanted interpretation of an issue that Boyles suggests has been previously badly slanted, in the opposite direction, by the 'politically correct'. Although it is easy to dismiss such an article on a number of grounds (not least of which is the nature of the magazine in which it appeared), it does reflect how extreme some views of sexual harassment have become. Here it is represented as a problem for men, for whom the courtship ritual has become even more dangerous.

Interpretations such as these have become commonplace in recent years. In many cases writers infer motives for behaviour that shift the identity of the victim onto the misunderstood 'alleged' harasser. In part, this is possible because existing definitions of sexual harassment omit one simple consideration—a motive for harassment. By concentrating on defining a range of unacceptable behaviours, and then shifting the responsibility for interpretation onto the observer (the victim), issues of intention are almost completely ignored. In the absence of any reason for *why* a person has behaved in a particular way, we make inferences based on our own beliefs and attitudes. Not surprisingly, a writer for *Playboy* infers that women are making life harder for innocent men.

Until legislation makes some attempt to address the issue of intention, this situation is likely to persist, for the simple reason that people are unsure as to why such behaviour takes place. We do not interpret events in isolation, but need to understand why something has happened. We need to infer a motive for an action. Knowing why something happened is crucial to understanding it and then taking appropriate action to prevent it.

The other aspect of such an initiative would be that the emphasis on the victim's interpretation needs to be reconsidered. As there is no universal standard of 'uncomfortableness', it is left to 'reasonable' people to decide on whether a victim's claims are justified. By failing to even define what might constitute a reasonable standard, legislation leaves itself open to accusations of subjectivity and, consequently, inconsistency. Neither characteristic can be the basis for effective legislation.

Redefining sexual harassment

In Chapter 2 we attempted the process of 'deconstructing' the term *sexual harassment*. We now conclude this deconstruction by proposing that the term sexual harassment be broken down into a series of distinct behaviours that could form the basis of new legislation. This would involve the following:

1. Separate the offences of *rape* and *sexual assault* from *sexual harassment*

Rape and sexual assault are offences for which there are already established laws. They are two of the most serious criminal offences and it is wholly inappropriate that they be clustered together with other offences. Sexual harassment and rape may share some underlying causes, but they are distinct behaviours. As mentioned in Chapter 2, the inclusion of rape and sexual offences under the category of sexual harassment hinders theoretical understanding of the issue, since no theory can account for such a potentially diverse range of experiences. Another reason for the separation of the terms is that it would be inappropriate to take action against a rapist by using legislation designed primarily to protect women from discrimination.

2. Abandon the term *sexual harassment*

We propose that the term *sexual harassment* be abandoned and that it be replaced with a series of distinct offences or descriptions that reflect the underlying causes of the behaviours currently labelled as sexual harassment. These include:

Sexual extortion

This is otherwise known as *quid pro quo* harassment. It is the most salient type of sexual harassment behaviour. To many people, this form of harassment *is* sexual harassment. Sexual extortion is a behaviour that observers (male and female) almost unanimously agree constitutes sexual harassment. When a person uses their organisational power to make sexual demands of another then the perceptions of the victim are largely irrelevant.

Sexual discrimination

Many sexual harassment behaviours are intended to discriminate against one section of the workforce. For example, displaying nude pin-ups in public areas is intended to remind the women present of their sex roles, and that they are not part of the dominant workgroup (the men). Such behaviours help to create a climate in which the targeted workers are made to feel uncomfortable or intimidated. Legislation against sexual harassment is often a component of sex discrimination, reflecting the underlying motives for such behaviours.

Bullying

Sometimes sexual harassment may be targeted at one or two individuals. This may be because of personal motives, rather than an attempt to discriminate against a whole section of the workforce. For example, a bully may attempt to isolate and intimidate one female worker, at the same time maintaining good relations with other women in the workplace.

Unwanted sexual attention

Organisations might also like to consider their position concerning a fourth category of behaviour—that of unwanted sexual attention. Some organisations prohibit romantic relationships between employees, although most remain more tolerant. It is likely to prove impossible to legislate against such behaviour, but there is very little reason to believe that any such legislation should be necessary. Men and women have been negotiating such issues for countless centuries and are likely to do so for the foreseeable future! The most significant complicating factor is when the unwanted suitor is a superior within an organisation. Clearly this issue would need to be addressed, but even then wholesale bans are likely to provoke outcries of unnecessary interference and to prove ineffective.

In summary then, we propose that the existing definition of sexual harassment be broken down into five main components. These are:

- rape and sexual assault
- sexual extortion
- sexual discrimination
- bullying
- unwanted romantic relationships.

Adopting such categories would help organisations convey to their employees a greater understanding of why harassment occurs and its effects on workers. By taking a proactive role in tackling such issues, firms will convey to their workers genuine concern for their safety and well-being. It also provides a framework for understanding why a person is harassing another, and may suggest possible remedies.

Although we have come a long way in trying to deal with sexual harassment over the last 20 years, there is little to reason to be complacent about what has been achieved. Like Frankenstein's monster, legislation and policies have been bolted together from whatever pieces have been available, and the weaknesses in the joints are still showing. The only way forward is for specifically designed legislation to be drafted. While governments ponder such issues, the responsibility to take action has been placed with organisations. Hopefully *Sexual Harassment* will have contributed to a greater understanding of why sexual harassment occurs, and to show that there are a number of steps that organisations can take to ensure that it is either minimised or eliminated.

appendix one

The Sexual Harassment in the Workplace Inventory (SHWI)

Sexual Behaviour in the Workplace Survey

The aim of this survey is to find out about *unwelcome sexual behaviours* that may be present in the workplace.

In the following pages there are a series of questions about behaviours that were directed at you, or may have happened in your working environment. Before you complete the survey, there are a few points that you should remember:

1.   The questions start with 'Has anyone at work…'. 'Anyone at work' means any person you regularly work with, or someone you come into contact with in a work context (such as clients, customers or contract workers). That person may be your superior/boss/supervisor, co-worker or subordinate. More than one person may have committed the behaviours in question.
2.   Only answer *Yes* to questions concerning behaviours that occurred *within the last year* and/or *within your current organisation/company*.
3.   Please refer to these notes if you have any doubts about answering *Yes* or *No* to the questions.

PLEASE NOTE: This survey is anonymous and all information collected is confidential. Please do not identify yourself.

Part 1: Offensive, humiliating or embarrassing sexual behaviours

In this section there are questions about *unwelcome sexual* behaviours that *you personally* may have experienced. *Unwelcome* means that you found the behaviours to be offensive, humiliating or embarrassing. If you experienced any of these behaviours and found them unwelcome, circle the *Yes* response.

If the behaviours happened but you did not consider them unwelcome, then answer *No*.

In your current job…

1. Has someone at work given or shown you (for example, left in your desk) sexual items, such as pornographic materials, underwear, or condoms? Only answer *Yes* if the materials were shown or given *directly* to you.

Circle one: No   Yes

2. Has someone at work invaded your personal space, cornered you or chased you?

                               No   Yes

3. Has someone at work eyed you up/ogled/leered at you?

                               No   Yes

4. Has someone at work touched/tickled/stroked/brushed against you, or attempted to do so?

                               No   Yes

5. Has someone at work grabbed/pinched/fondled/kissed you, or attempted to do so?

                               No   Yes

6. Has someone at work *sexually* assaulted you, or attempted to do so?

                               No   Yes

7.   Has someone at work made sexual gestures directly to you (such as pretending to masturbate or flash)?

No   Yes

8.   Has someone at work made sexual remarks or comments *directly to you* (including phone calls and letters), such as sexual joking, sexual 'advice' or comments about sexual matters including your sexuality?

No   Yes

9.   Has someone at work made sexual remarks or comments *about you to other people* (you may have been present at the time), such as spreading rumours, making sexual jokes, offering sexual 'advice' or comments about sexual matters including your sexuality?

No   Yes

10.   Has someone at work *offered* you sexual favours in exchange for a work-related reward (such as promotion or a good reference)?

No   Yes

11.   Has someone at work made sexual requests of you (including sexual advances or propositions)?

No   Yes

12.   Has someone at work made sexual requests of you where you were offered some kind of work-related reward (such as preferential treatment or promotion) for engaging in sexual behaviour?

No   Yes

13.   Has someone at work made sexual requests of you where you were threatened with some kind of work-related punishment (such as sacking or demotion) if you refused to engage in sexual behaviour?

No   Yes

PART 2: Workplace atmosphere

In this section there are questions about behaviours that may occur in your workplace, which *you* find *unwelcome* and that contribute to an unpleasant working atmosphere.

These behaviours are *not* about you personally, although you may be one of the many people to whom the behaviour is directed.

Unwelcome means that you found the behaviours to be offensive, humiliating or embarrassing. If these behaviours happened in your workplace and you found them unwelcome, circle the *Yes* response. If the behaviours happened but you did not consider them unwelcome, then answer *No*.

14.   Has someone at work made comments *in public*, about any sexual matters, including sexual wishes?

Circle one   No   Yes

15.   Has someone at work made sexual remarks or comments *in public* about groups of people, such as men or women, gays or lesbians?

                                No   Yes

16.   Has someone at work *publicly* displayed sexual materials (such as pornography, underwear or condoms)?

                                  No   Yes

PART 3: Sexual harassment in the workplace

17.   Has anyone at work (in the last year and in your current organisation) sexually harassed you?

Circle one   No   Yes

If *yes*, please *briefly* describe the *behaviours* you experienced:

_____

_____

_____

PART 4: About yourself

In this section there are some questions about you and where you work. Please do not identify your company.

18.   Your sex.

Circle one   Male   Female

19.   What is your job title/profession or position? Please specify.

_____

20.   Are there more men or women in your department, division or section? Circle one

        Mostly men   Roughly equal numbers   Mostly women
                          of men and women

21.   Are there more men or women in your organisation as a whole?

        Mostly men   Roughly equal numbers   Mostly women
                          of men and women

22.   What *type* of organisation do you work for? Please specify.

_____

Sexual Harassment in the Workplace: A guide for employers

The following material comes from a booklet published by the UK Department of Education and Employment in February 1997. It provides a clear and useful overview of sexual harassment for employers. Naturally, its comments on legal requirements apply to the UK and not necessarily to other jurisdictions.

Introduction

Sexual harassment can be one of the most upsetting and humiliating experiences a person can suffer. When sexual harassment occurs at work, it can seriously affect the confidence of your employees and consequently how well they do their jobs. It can also affect their physical and mental health and lead to absenteeism.

Not all—possibly not many—people who are sexually harassed know what to do about it. Many suffer in silence; some may even feel compelled to leave their jobs. Whatever the outcome, sexual harassment is bad for your company's morale and bad for business efficiency.

This booklet offers guidance on how to deal with this difficult problem. It outlines good practice which is consistent with the European Commission's recommended Code of Practice, and draws on advice from the Department for Education and Employment's Advisory Committee on Women's Employment whose members include representatives of the CBI, TUC and the main political parties, the Chair of the Equal Opportunities Commission and a number of independent members with experience of equal opportunities issues.

No one should have to put up with sexual harassment—neither employer or employee. Having a clear policy to deal with the problem can be the most effective preventative measure an employer can take to avoid a costly and upsetting complaint. So whatever your business, please read this booklet.

What is sexual harassment?

There is no hard and fast definition of sexual harassment—many people have different views about where the boundaries lie. In the European Commission's Code of Practice, sexual harassment is broadly described as 'unwanted conduct of a sexual nature, or other conduct based on sex affecting the dignity of women and men at work'. Most people who are sexually harassed are women, but it is important to remember that it can happen to men too.

Examples of conduct which are clearly unacceptable include:

- unwelcome sexual attention
- subjecting someone to insults or ridicule because of their sex
- suggestions that sexual favours may further someone's career (or that refusal may damage it)
- basing decisions affecting an employee's career on willingness or refusal to offer sexual favours.

Sexual harassment can also extend to other forms of behaviour which may offend, such as lewd, suggestive or overfamiliar behaviour and display or circulation of sexually suggestive material.

Sexual harassment can be persistent, unwanted sexual attention which continues after the person receiving it makes clear that they want it to stop. However a single incident can also constitute sexual harassment if it is sufficiently serious.

Conduct which may amount to sexual harassment is often not intended to cause offence but occurs because of a lack of awareness to other people's feelings.

Sexual harassment and the law

In certain circumstances sexual harassment may be unlawful, and under the Sex Discrimination Act 1975 (UK) employers may be vicariously liable for the actions of their employees unless they can prove that they took such steps as were reasonably practicable to prevent the employees doing the act or acts complained of.

It is also an offence under the Criminal Justice and Public Order Act 1994 (UK) to intentionally cause harassment, harm or distress through using threatening, abusive or insulting words, behaviour or displays. Conviction attracts a fine/prison or both.

Preventing sexual harassment

It could happen in your organisation

It is in everyone's interest for there to be a working environment which encourages harmonious, respectful and dignified working relations between the sexes—a situation which probably exists in most organisations.

But do not assume sexual harassment is not a problem in your organisation just because you have not had any complaints. It may be that your employees:

- feel that there is no point in making a complaint as no action will be taken
- do not know to whom they should complain
- may be too embarrassed to make a complaint (most people who have been sexually harassed do not want attention drawn to the situation, they just want the harassment to stop)
- do not want the person harassing them to get into serious trouble
- do not want to be forced to the extreme of leaving their job or taking the complaint to an industrial tribunal
- fear reprisals for making a complaint.

Appendix two

Draw up a policy

Prevention is better than cure. A well thought out policy on sexual harassment should be a normal part of good personnel and resource management as well as of equal opportunity practices. It is sensible to establish a set of basic standards which all of your employees know about and are expected to conform to.

A formal policy making clear that all employees have the right to be treated with dignity and respect, and that sexual harassment at work is not to be permitted or condoned can be a valuable deterrent. It can also give reassurance to all your staff who disapprove of sexual harassment but feel uncomfortable about speaking out. For maximum impact it is desirable for the policy statement to:

- set out what is inappropriate behaviour at work
- make clear that sexual harassment may be treated as a disciplinary offence with appropriate penalties
- explain that such behaviour may in certain circumstances be unlawful
- make clear that all employees have a responsibility to comply with the policy and to treat colleagues of both sexes with dignity and respect
- describe how to complain about sexual harassment and how to get help
- assure your staff that allegations of sexual harassment will be dealt with seriously and confidentially—and that they need not fear victimisation for making or being involved in a complaint
- make it the duty of your supervisors and managers to implement the policy and bring it to the attention of their staff.

It is important that any policy statement is regularly and clearly communicated to employees so they are aware of their right to complain, and know to whom to complain and that their complaint will be dealt with fairly and quickly. Where appropriate, you may wish to consult with your employees or their representatives about the statement.

Training

Managers and supervisors may need training to help them be alert to the possibility of sexual harassment in their work area, know how to respond to complaints and how to use agreed procedures.

It is also a good idea to include details of your policy on sexual harassment, and of procedures for dealing with complaints, in induction and training programs for all staff.

Monitoring

Once the policy has been decided and put into effect it is a good idea to have regular reviews to see how effective it is and whether improvements are needed.

The above measures show what you as an employer can do. Many have been adopted by organisations who are giving a lead in this field.

Of course, you may not have the resources to implement them in full. You may need to adapt some of the practical steps to your own needs and circumstances, particularly if you are a small or medium-sized organisation.

You can get advice about what to do from the Equal Opportunities Commission. More general advice may be sought from the Advisory Conciliation and Arbitration Service (ACAS) (See Appendix III).

Dealing with complaints of sexual harassment

What do you do when you receive a complaint

Once a complaint has been made it should not be ignored. If it is not investigated an employer may have little defence if the complaint proceeds to an industrial tribunal. The investigation can be carried out informally or formally but in any event you should act quickly and ensure that the investigation is independent and objective and undertaken by someone with sufficient authority to take appropriate action.

Informal procedures to resolve a complaint

It is obviously better for a complaint to be resolved informally if possible. In many cases it may be sufficient for you, or someone acting on your behalf, to explain to the person causing offence that the behaviour complained of is unwelcome, embarrassing and is interfering with work.

Formal procedures to resolve a complaint

If informal attempts have not been successful or the behaviour is too serious for the problem to be resolved informally, the matter should be pursued through a formal complaints procedure. This will require:

- the parties to be identified
- a thorough and impartial investigation of all the evidence
- each side to have an opportunity to put their side of the case, either on their own or with a friend or employee representative or some other appropriate person
- consideration to be given to imposing a disciplinary penalty if it is found that sexual harassment did occur.

Subsequent action

If a complaint is upheld you may need to separate the parties involved. However, it is important to insure that the complainant is not adversely affected by the action taken.

If the complaint is not upheld, you may still wish to separate the complainant and the other person involved in the interests of harmonious staff relations.

In any case where a complaint is upheld it is important to check that the harassment has stopped and that there has been no victimisation, otherwise you may be liable in law for any subsequent acts of harassment.

Help for employees

People who have been sexually harassed need to be aware of what steps to take...

Advice and counselling

Wherever possible, a person who has complained about sexual harassment should have access to someone who can give them sympathetic advice and, if necessary, counselling. This should take place in an atmosphere of total confidentiality and without pressure to take the complaint further.

If you have the resources, designating a specific person to act as counsellor who could perhaps help to resolve the problem informally may be of assistance. The counsellor could be a member of the personnel or welfare department and may require training to increase their understanding of the problem and how to deal with it. Counselling arrangements should not interfere with normal industrial relations procedures and should, where appropriate, be agreed with your employees or their representatives. If you are a large enough organisation you may be able to designate persons from both sexes to act as counsellors. Where counselling is available, it is of course essential to provide space for any interviews and conversations to take place in private.

Annex: Sexual harassment and the law

What follows is not intended to be a complete and authoritative statement of the law. In a particular case you may need to seek legal advice.

Sex Discrimination Act 1975 (UK)

Under GB law sexual harassment at work may amount to unlawful sex discrimination under the Sex Discrimination Act 1975 (SDA) which provides that a person discriminates directly against a woman if 'on the ground of her sex he treats

her less favourably than he treats or would treat a man' in comparable circumstances. (The Act also covers discrimination against men.)

In the landmark case of *Porcelli* v. *Strathclyde Regional Council*, the Scot-
tish Court of Appeal ruled that a woman who complained of sexual harassment had
suffered unlawful sex discrimination. In that case, a woman was resented by two of
her male colleagues who pursued a policy of vindictive unpleasantness towards her
over a period to make her apply for a transfer to another post, which she eventually
did. Their conduct included personal insults, obscene language, suggestive remarks,
brushing up against her, and intimidation. She won her case against her employer
under the SDA. Since then there have been an increasing number of sexual
harassment cases under the SDA covering a range of different kinds of conduct,
ranging from relatively minor to very serious.

To be successful under the SDA a complainant will have to show that the
harassment has caused them a 'detriment', that is a disadvantage of some kind. This
is likely to be clear where, for example, the conduct causes the person to resign or
seek a transfer, or affects their health.

Under the SDA, employers are not only responsible for their own conduct
but are also liable for any discriminatory acts committed by their employees in the
course of employment—whether or not committed with the employer's knowledge
or approval. An employer will escape such liability only if he or she took such steps
as were reasonably practicable to prevent the employee doing the act or acts
complained of.

The SDA also protects people who make complaints about breaches of the
Act, and anyone else who gives evidence in support of a complaint, against any
subsequent victimisation by their employer.

Unfair discrimination

A complaint of unfair dismissal under the Employment Rights Act 1996 (UK) may
be available in two particular situations, assuming the person had the necessary
qualifying period of employment. First, where a person has been dismissed; for

example, a person who was dismissed because they objected to conduct they found unacceptable could complain that the dismissal was unfair. Second, where a person has resigned because of conduct by the employer which is a fundamental breach of contract (this is called 'constructive dismissal'); for example, failure by an employer to make an adequate investigation of an allegation of serious sexual harassment has been held to be conduct entitling an employee to resign and bring a complaint of 'constructive dismissal'.

Other legal consequences

Certain acts of sexual harassment may amount to unlawful assault, giving rise to civil or criminal liability. In particular, indecent assault is a serious criminal offence.

Where sexual harassment results in injury to an employee's health or places them under considerable stress, the employer might be held to be in breach of health and safety duties—or of other legal duties owed to their employees—if the employer was aware of the situation (or should have been) and took no steps to prevent it.

Remedies

People who think the treatment they have suffered amounts to unlawful sex discrimination or who have grounds for claiming they have been unfairly dismissed, may present a complaint to an industrial tribunal. In either case where the tribunal finds the complaint well-founded it has the power to award compensation. In cases alleging sex discrimination, complaints to tribunals must normally be made within three months of the act complained of; in cases alleging unfair dismissal, they must be made within three months of the effective date of termination of employment.

European Community law

Sexual harassment at work may, in certain circumstances, be contrary to the principal of equal treatment for men and women laid down in EC law. This principal is given effect in GB law by the *Sex Discrimination Act* 1975 (see above).

Equal Opportunities Commission's (EOC's) Code of Practice

The EOC's Code of Practice recommends that employers establish proper standards of conduct and behaviour in their organisations, and also take particular care in dealing with allegations of sexual harassment. The Code is admissible in any tribunal proceedings under the SDA, and the tribunal must take into account any provision of the Code which it thinks relevant to the issues in the case before it.

appendix three

Useful addresses

Australia

National
Human Rights and Equal Opportunity
Commission (HREOC) National Office
Level 8, Piccadilly Tower
133 Castlereagh Street
Sydney NSW 2000
GPO Box 5218
Sydney 2001
Tel: 1800 021 199

New South Wales

Anti-Discrimination Board

Sydney
Level 4, 181 Lawson Street
Redfern NSW 2016
Tel: (02) 9318 5400

Wollongong
84 Crown Street
Wollongong NSW 2500
Tel: (042) 268 190

Appendix three

Newcastle
79 Hunter Street
Newcastle NSW 2300
Tel: (049) 264 300

Queensland

Anti-Discrimination Commission/ HREOC
Regional Offices

Brisbane
Ground Floor, QNU Building
27 Peel Street
South Brisbane QLD 4101
PO Box 5363
West End QLD 4101
Tel: 1800 177 822 (QLD only)

Rockhampton
3rd Floor, MLC House
130 Victoria Parade
Rockhampton, QLD 4700
PO Box 1390
Rockhampton QLD 4700
Tel: 1800 804 288

Cairns
2nd Floor, Aplin House
19 Aplin Street,
PO Box 375
Cairns QLD 4870
Tel: 1800 803 271

Tasmania

HREOC Regional Office
Suite 4, Ground Floor, City Mill
11–13 Morrison Street
Hobart TAS 7000
Tel: 1800 001 222

Northern Territory

HREOC Regional Office
1st Floor, TCG Centre
80 Mitchell Street
Darwin NT 0800
LMB 4 GPO
Darwin NT 0801
Tel: (089) 819 111

Anti-Discrimination Commission
National Mutual Building
7–11 Cavenagh Street
Darwin 0800
LMB 22
GPO Darwin 0801
Tel: (089) 813 813

Australian Capital Territory

Human Rights Office
Level 2, Comcare Building
40 Allara Street
Canberra ACT 2608
Tel: (06) 247 3002

Victoria

Equal Opportunity Commission
Level 3, 380 Lonsdale Street
Melbourne VIC 3000
Tel: 1800 134 142 (VIC only)

South Australia

Commissioner for Equal Opportunity
Ground Floor, Wakefield House
30 Wakefield Street
Adelaide SA 5000
Tel: 1800 188 163

Western Australia

Equal Opportunity Commission
1st Floor, Capita Building
5 Mill Street
Perth WA 6000
Tel: 1800 198 149

United Kingdom

England

The Equal Opportunities Commission
Overseas House
Quay Street
Manchester M3 3HN
Tel: (0161) 833 9244

Scotland

The Equal Opportunities Commission
Stock Exchange House
7 Nelson Mandela Place
Glasgow G2 1QW
Tel: (0141) 248 5833

Wales

The Equal Opportunities Commission
Caerwys House
Windsor Lane
Cardiff CF1 1LB
Tel: (01222) 343 552

Copies of 'Sexual Harassment in the Workplace: A
guide for employers' (PL923) cited in Appendix Two
are available from:

Cambertown Ltd
Unit 8, Commercial Road
Goldthorpe Industrial Estate
Goldthorpe
Rotherham S63 9BL
Tel: (01709) 888 688

More general advice may be sought from the
Advisory, Conciliation and Arbitration Service
(ACAS)
Head Office
Brandon House
180 Borough High Street
London SE1 1LW
Tel: (0171) 210 3000

bibliography

Abbey, A. (1982) 'Sex differences in attributions for friendly behavior: Do males misperceive females' friendliness?', *Journal of Personality and Social Psychology*, vol. 42, no. 5, pp. 830–8.

A guide to the 1992 amendments to the Sex Discrimination Act 1984 (1993) Human Rights and Equal Opportunity Commission, Australian Government Publishing Service: Canberra.

Backhouse, C. and Cohen, L. (1982) *Sexual Harassment on the Job. How to Avoid the Working Woman's Nightmare,* Englewood Cliffs, New Jersey: Prentice-Hall.

Baker, D. D., Terpstra, D. E. and Cutler, B. D. (1990) 'Perceptions of sexual harassment: A re-examination of gender differences', *The Journal of Psychology*, vol. 124, no. 4, pp. 409–16.

Bartling, C. A. and Eisenman, R. (1993) 'Sexual harassment proclivities in men and women', *Bulletin of the Psychonomic Society*, 31, 3, pp. 189–92.

Barton, L. and Eichelberger, J. (1994) 'Sexual harassment: Assessing the need for corporate policies in the workplace', *Executive Development*, vol. 7, no. 1, pp. 24–8.

Benson, D. J and Thomson, G. E. (1982) 'Sexual harassment on a university campus: The confluence of authority relations, sexual interest and gender stratification', *Social Problems,* vol. 29, no. 3, pp. 236–51.

Boyles, D. (1991) 'The thinking man's guide to working with women', *Playboy,* pp. 116–18, 156–60.

Cleveland, J. (1994) 'Women and sexual harassment: Work and well-being in US organizations', in M. Davidson and R. Burke (eds.) *Women in Management: Current Research Issues*, London: Paul Chapman.

Cleveland, J. and Kerst, M. (1993) 'Sexual harassment and perceptions of power: An under-articulated relationship', *Journal of Vocational Behavior*, vol. 42, pp. 49–67.

Collins, E. G. C. and Blodgett, T. B. (1981) 'Sexual harassment: Some see it… some won't', *Harvard Business Review,* March–April, pp. 76–95.

Concise Oxford Dictionary (1995) 9th edn, Oxford: Oxford University Press.

Crull, P. (1982) 'Stress effects of sexual harassment on the job: Implications for counselling', *American Journal of Orthopsychiatry*, vol. 52, pp. 539–44.

Davidson, M. and Earnshaw, J. (1990) 'Policies, practices and attitudes towards sexual harassment in UK organisations', *Personnel Review*, vol. 19, no. 3, pp. 23–7.

Dziech, B. W. and Weiner, L. (1990) *The Lecherous Professor: Sexual harassment on campus*, 2nd edn, Urbana, Illinois: University of Illinois Press.

Equal Employment Opportunity Commission (1980) 'Guidelines on discrimination because of sex', *Federal Register,* 45, pp. 74676–7.

Equal Employment Opportunity Commission (1993) 'Interim guidelines on workplace harassment', *Federal Register*, 58, p. 51266.

Farley, L. (1978) *Sexual Shakedown: The Sexual Harassment of Women on the Job,* New York: Warner Books.

Fitzgerald, L. F. (1994) *No safe haven: Violence against women at home, at work, and in the community,* Washington, DC: American Psychological Association.

— (1990) 'Sexual harassment: The definition and measurement of a construct', in M. A. Paludi (ed.), *Ivory Power: Sexual Harassment on Campus,* Albany, New York: SUNY Press.

— (1993) 'Sexual harassment: A research analysis and agenda for the 1990s', *Journal of Vocational Behavior*, vol. 42, pp. 5–27.

Fitzgerald, L. F., Gold, Y. and Brock, K. F. (date unknown) Women's responses to victimization: Validation of an objective inventory to assess strategies for responding to sexual harassment, unpublished manuscript, in possession of the Department of Psychology, University of Illinois, Champaign.

Fitzgerald, L. F., Gold, Y., Ormerod, A. J. and Weitzman, L. (1988) 'Academic harassment: Sex and denial in scholarly garb', *Psychology of Women Quarterly*, vol. 12, pp. 329–40.

Fitzgerald, L. F., Shullman, S. L., *et. al.* (1988) 'The incidence and dimensions of sexual harassment in academia and the workplace', *Journal of Vocational Behavior*, vol. 32, pp. 152–75.

Franklin, P., Moglen, H., Zatlin-Boring, P. and Angress, R. (1981) *Sexual and Gender Harassment in the Academy: A guide for faculty, students, and administrators*, New York: Modern Language Association of America.

Grauerholz, E. (1989) 'Sexual harassment of women professors by students: Exploring the dynamics of power, authority and gender in a university setting', *Sex Roles*, vol. 21, pp. 789–801.

Gruber, J. (1992) 'A typology of personal and environmental sexual harassment: Research and policy implications for the 1990s', *Sex Roles*, vol. 26, no. 11/12, pp. 447–64.

Gruber, J. and Bjorn, L. (1986) 'Women's responses to sexual harassment: An analysis of sociocultural, organizational, and personal resource models', *Social Science Quarterly*, pp. 814–26.

Gutek, B. A. (1985) *Sex and the Workplace,* San Francisco: Jossey-Bass.

Gutek, B. A and Jensen, I. (1982) 'Attributions and assignment of responsibility in sexual harassment', *Journal of Social Issues*, vol. 38, no. 4, pp. 121–36.

Gutek, B. A. and Koss, M. P. (1993) 'Changed women and changed organizations: Consequences of and coping with sexual harassment', *Journal of Vocational Behavior*, vol. 42, pp. 28–48.

Gutek, B. A. and Morasch, B. (1982) 'Sex-ratios, sex-role spillover and sexual harassment of women at work', *Journal of Social Issues*, vol. 38, no. 4, pp. 55–74.

'It's time to stop sexual harassment', (No date), University of New South Wales, Sydney.

Kanter, R. M. (1977) 'Some effects of proportions in group life: Skewed sex ratios and response to token women', *American Journal of Sociology*, vol. 2, no. 5, pp. 965–90.

Lafontaine, E. and Tredeau, L. (1986) 'The frequency, sources and correlates of sexual harassment among women in traditional male occupations', *Sex Roles*, vol. 15, pp. 433–42.

Loy, P. and Stewart, L. (1984) 'The extent and effects of the sexual harassment of working women', *Sociological Focus*, vol. 17, pp. 31–43.

MacKinnon, C. (1979) *Sexual Harassment of Working Women,* New Haven, Connecticut: Yale University Press.

Malamuth, N. (1981) 'Rape proclivity among males', *Journal of Social Issues*, vol. 37, pp. 520–47.

Nixon, S. and Roberts, J. (1992) *Dealing with Sexual Harassment*, Melbourne: Ron Hannan Print Works.

Petrocelli, W. and Repa, B. K. (1992) *Sexual harassment on the job,* Berkeley, California: Nolo Press.

Pryor, J. B. (1987) 'Sexual harassment proclivities in men', *Sex Roles*, vol. 5, no. 6, pp. 269–90.

Pryor, J. B., LaVite, C. M. and Stoller, L. M. (1993) 'A social psychological analysis of sexual harassment: The person/situations interaction', *Journal of Vocational Behavior*, vol. 42, pp. 68–83.

Reilly, M., Carpenter, S., Dull, V. and Bartlett, K. (1982) 'The factorial survey technique: An approach to defining sexual harassment on campus', *Journal of Social Issues*, vol. 38, pp. 99–110.

Roiphe, K. (1994) *The Morning After: Sex, Fear and Feminism*, London: Hamish Hamilton.

Safran, C. (1976) 'What men do to women on the job', *Redbook,* November, pp. 217–23.

Sandroff, R. (1988) 'Sexual harassment in the Fortune 500', *Working Woman,* December, pp. 69–73.

Sex Discrimination Act 1984 (Cth).

Sexual harassment of women at work: A study from West Yorkshire (1983) Leeds Trade Union and Community Resource Information Centre,York: TUCRIC Publications Ltd.

Soutar, G. N., Savery, L. K. and Dufty, N. F. (1987) 'Sexual harassment in the banking industry: Some Australian evidence', *Human Resource Management Australia*, November, pp. 82–8.

Stockdale, J. (1986) Sexual harassment in a university setting, paper presented at the London Conference of the British Psychological Society, December.

Stringer, D., Remick, H., Salisbury, J. and Ginorio, A. (1990) 'The power and reasons behind sexual harassment: An employer's guide to solutions', *Public Personnel Management*, vol. 19, no. 1, Spring, pp. 43–52.

Tangri, S., Burt, M. and Johnson, L. (1982) 'Sexual harassment at work: Three explanatory models', *Journal of Social Issues*, vol. 38, no. 4, pp. 33–54.

Terpstra, D. E. and Baker, D. D. (1989) 'The identification and classification of reactions to sexual harassment', *Journal of Organizational Behavior*, vol. 10, pp. 1–14.

Terpstra, D. E. and Cook, S. E. (1985) 'Complainant characteristics and reported behaviors and consequences associated with formal sexual harassment charges', *Personnel Psychology*, vol. 38, pp. 559–74.

Till, F. (1980) 'Sexual Harassment: A report on the sexual harassment of students', Washington, DC: National Advisory Council on Women's Educational Programs.

United States Merit Systems Protection Board (1988) *Sexual Harassment in the Federal Government: An Update.* Washington, DC: US Government Printing Office.

United States Merit Systems Protection Board (1981) *Sexual Harassment in the Federal Workplace: Is it a Problem?*, Washington, DC: US Government Printing Office.

Wilson, K. R. and Krauss, L. A. (1983) 'Sexual harassment in the university', *Journal of College Student Personnel*, vol. 24, pp. 219–24.

Working Women United Institute (1978) 'Sexual Harassment on the Job: Questions and Answers', New York: WWUI.

Zalk, S. R. (1990) 'Men in the academy: A psychological profile of harassment', in M. A. Paludi (ed.) *Ivory Power: Sexual Harassment on Campus*, New York: SUNY Press.

Index